1st EDITION

Perspectives on Diseases and Disorders

Epilepsy

Mary E. Williams
Book Editor

Detroit • New York • San Francisco • New Haven, Conn • Waterville, Maine • London

Christine Nasso, *Publisher*
Elizabeth Des Chenes, *Managing Editor*

© 2010 Greenhaven Press, a part of Gale, Cengage Learning

LIBRARY OF CONGRESS CATALOGING-IN-PUBLICATION DATA

Epilepsy / Mary E. Williams, book editor.
    p. cm. -- (Perspectives on diseases and disorders)
  Includes bibliographical references and index.
  ISBN 978-0-7377-4552-8 (hardcover)
 1. Epilepsy. I. Williams, Mary E., 1960-
  RC372.E6515 2009
  616.8'53--dc22

          2009022930

Printed in the United States of America
1 2 3 4 5 6 7 13 12 11 10 09

CONTENTS

FOREWORD

"Medicine, to produce health, has to examine disease."
—Plutarch

Independent research on a health issue is often the first step to complement discussions with a physician. But locating accurate, well-organized, understandable medical information can be a challenge. A simple Internet search on terms such as "cancer" or "diabetes," for example, returns an intimidating number of results. Sifting through the results can be daunting, particularly when some of the information is inconsistent or even contradictory. The Greenhaven Press series Perspectives on Diseases and Disorders offers a solution to the often overwhelming nature of researching diseases and disorders.

From the clinical to the personal, titles in the Perspectives on Diseases and Disorders series provide students and other researchers with authoritative, accessible information in unique anthologies that include basic information about the disease or disorder, controversial aspects of diagnosis and treatment, and first-person accounts of those impacted by the disease. The result is a well-rounded combination of primary and secondary sources that, together, provide the reader with a better understanding of the disease or disorder.

Each volume in Perspectives on Diseases and Disorders explores a particular disease or disorder in detail. Material for each volume is carefully selected from a wide range of sources, including encyclopedias, journals, newspapers, nonfiction books, speeches, government documents, pamphlets, organization newsletters, and position papers. Articles in the first chapter provide an authoritative, up-to-date overview that covers symptoms, causes and effects, treatments, cures, and medical advances. The second chapter presents a substantial number of opposing viewpoints on controversial treatments and other current debates relating to the volume topic. The third chapter offers a variety of personal perspectives on the disease or disorder. Patients, doctors, caregivers, and loved ones represent just some of the voices found in this narrative chapter.

Each Perspectives on Diseases and Disorders volume also includes:

- An **annotated table of contents** that provides a brief summary of each article in the volume.
- An **introduction** specific to the volume topic.
- Full-color **charts and graphs** to illustrate key points, concepts, and theories.
- Full-color **photos** that show aspects of the disease or disorder and enhance textual material.
- **"Fast Facts"** that highlight pertinent additional statistics and surprising points.
- A **glossary** providing users with definitions of important terms.
- A **chronology** of important dates relating to the disease or disorder.
- An annotated list of **organizations to contact** for students and other readers seeking additional information.
- A **bibliography** of additional books and periodicals for further research.
- A detailed **subject index** that allows readers to quickly find the information they need.

Whether a student researching a disorder, a patient recently diagnosed with a disease, or an individual who simply wants to learn more about a particular disease or disorder, a reader who turns to Perspectives on Diseases and Disorders will find a wealth of information in each volume that offers not only basic information, but also vigorous debate from multiple perspectives.

INTRODUCTION

In 2005 Charley Williams Jr. was a soldier in the U.S. Army's 467th Engineer Battalion, fighting in the front lines of the Iraq War. The mission of his Trailblazer team was to search for roadside bombs, the leading threat to troops at that time. On March 27 Williams was at his station, manning a machine gun atop a Humvee at the head of a nine-vehicle convoy, when his driver turned slightly to avoid a pothole. "He veered off into the gravel and 'Ka-boom!'" Williams recalls. "The sound was so traumatic. It was like hitting a wall. I thought I was dead. I had shrapnel in my forehead. . . . Road debris just rained on top of me for probably three minutes."

Williams spent more than a year in military hospitals and rehabilitation facilities recuperating from multiple injuries before returning home. The explosion left him deaf in one ear and with limited use of his right arm. He is on nine prescription medications for anxiety, post-traumatic stress disorder, and chronic pain. Moreover, a traumatic brain injury (TBI) gives him frequent headaches and makes him forgetful to the point of needing directions from the Memphis Veterans Medical Center to his parents' home. This injury also places him at greatly increased risk of developing post-traumatic epilepsy years—or even decades—in the future.

Williams is not alone in his predicament. Traumatic brain injury has been identified as the "signature injury" of the wars in Iraq and Afghanistan, with an estimated ten thousand new cases of TBI over the past decade, according to the Department of Veterans Affairs. And about 150,000 U.S. veterans overall—including those who served in the Korean and Vietnam wars—have been diagnosed with

An Iraq War veteran works with a speech pathologist to overcome disabilities due to a traumatic brain injury. According to the Department of Veterans Affairs there have been ten thousand new cases reported since the Iraq War started. (AP Images)

TBI. Furthermore, the American Epilepsy Society notes that "posttraumatic epilepsy developed in over 50 percent of TBI victims with penetrating head injury in both the Korean and Vietnam Wars. While the long-term consequences of the new type of TBI encountered [in the Iraq and Afghanistan Wars] is not known, the potential for development of . . . epilepsy in [large numbers of Iraq] veterans with non-penetrating as well as penetrating head injury is significant."

Epilepsy is a family of brain disorders in which clusters of brain neurons flash out abnormal signals that cause seizures. A seizure may be mild, moderate, or severe, with symptoms ranging from eyelid fluttering and facial twitching to muscle rigidity, spasms, violent convulsions, and loss of consciousness. Affecting one out of one hundred people, the origins of 50 to 70 percent of epilepsy cases are unknown. Genetic factors and chemical imbalances in the brain may play a role; the disorder may also emerge because of brain damage caused by developmental deficiencies, tumors, toxins, and other illnesses. But one of the more traceable causes of epilepsy is head trauma resulting from car accidents, sports injuries, gunshot wounds, and combat injuries. Increased awareness about this potential source of epilepsy, experts maintain, could someday lead to better treatments for—and possibly the prevention of—this disorder.

Recent research suggests, for example, that some of the newer antiseizure drugs might prevent epilepsy in some people with TBIs if they start treatment with these medicines early in the healing process. However, an injured brain often experiences a "silent period" free of seizures before epilepsy emerges. Because the early symptoms of post-traumatic epilepsy are often subtle or unrecognized, many people at risk for the disorder lack the awareness that might encourage them to take advantage of preventative strategies.

These troubling facts about TBI and epilepsy lend urgency to the plight of recently injured veterans like Charley Williams. As neurologist John Booss explained in his 2007 statement before the Senate Committee on Veterans' Affairs:

> We do not have data on post-traumatic epilepsy from the current conflicts [but] the statistics from the Vietnam era are alarming. VA-funded research . . . found that 53 percent of veterans who suffered a penetrating TBI in Vietnam developed epilepsy within 15 years. . . . The relative risk for developing epilepsy more than 10 or 15 years after their injury was 25 times higher than their age-related civilian cohorts. Indeed, 15 percent did not manifest epilepsy until five or more years after their combat injury.

Booss maintains that the Veterans Administration (VA) lacks a much-needed national program for epilepsy with clear guidelines on when to refer patients for further assessment and treatment. Without such a program, many injured veterans are missing the window of opportunity during the early months after their trauma, when drugs or other still-developing treatments may help to avert epilepsy. He argues that Congress should authorize and strongly fund VA research, education, and clinical centers focused on preventing and treating post-traumatic epilepsy.

As epilepsy has various causes and forms, neurologists and other experts continue to examine myriad approaches to treating and managing the disorder. *Perspectives on Diseases and Disorders: Epilepsy* explores several of these

Members of Congress talk to the press on June 25, 2008, about the passage of the Americans with Disabilities Amendments Act to help veterans with post-traumatic brain injuries. (Kevin Dietsch/ UPI/Landov)

approaches, including the use of antiseizure drugs, surgery, electronic stimulation of the brain, dietary therapy, and trained seizure-response dogs. In addition, to enhance understanding about the personal and social impact of this disorder, this volume also includes narratives written by people living with epilepsy and caregivers for people with epilepsy. The perspectives in these chapters present a compelling overview of the challenges specific to this often misunderstood malady.

CHAPTER 1

Understanding Epilepsy

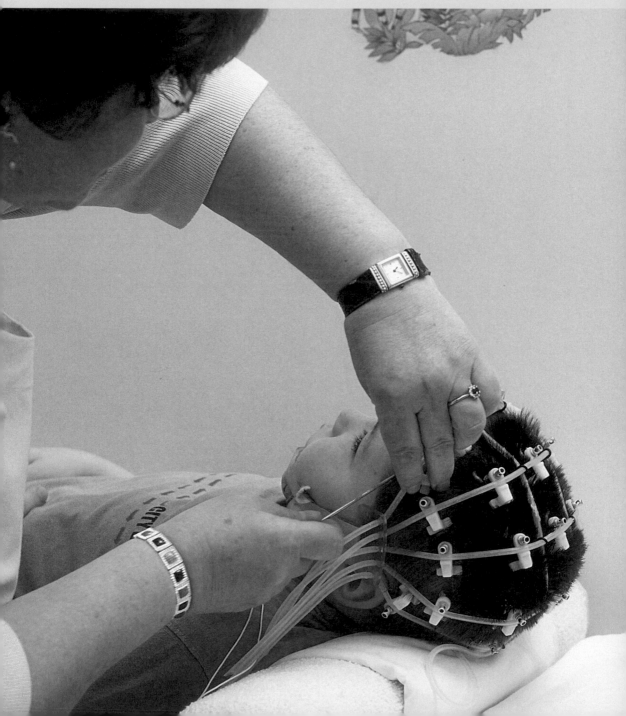

Epilepsy and Seizure Disorder: An Overview

Maureen Haggerty and Teresa G. Odle

In the following selection health writers Maureen Haggerty and Teresa G. Odle provide a general description of epilepsy, outlining the various types of epileptic seizures as well as possible causes, symptoms, and treatment options for this disorder. The seizures that characterize epilepsy result from abnormal electrical activity in the brain and may or may not include muscular convulsions and loss of consciousness. Anticonvulsant drugs are the most common form of epilepsy treatment, the authors explain, but surgery and special diets are options for those who are unable to control their seizures with medication. In addition, proper rest, balanced meals, and stress reduction can help to prevent seizures.

A seizure is a sudden disruption of the brain's normal electrical activity accompanied by altered consciousness and/or other neurological and behavioral manifestations. Epilepsy is a condition

SOURCE: Maureen Haggerty and Teresa G. Odle, *The Gale Encyclopedia of Medicine*, Belmont, CA: Gale, 2007. Copyright © 2008 Gale Cengage Learning. Reproduced by permission of Gale, a part of Cengage Learning.

Photo on facing page. A technician positions electrodes for an electroencephalogram (EEG) on a child's head to detect symptoms of epilepsy. (**BSIP/Photo Researchers Inc.**)

characterized by recurrent seizures that may include repetitive muscle jerking called convulsions.

There are more than 20 different seizure disorders. One in ten Americans will have a seizure at some time during their lifetime. More than 3 million Americans are affected by seizures.

Epilepsy affects 1–2% of the population of the United States. About 2.7 million Americans have active epilepsy, meaning that in the past 5 years they have had a seizure or been on medication for epilepsy. Epilepsy becomes more prevalent with increased age. About 1% of people under age 20 have epilepsy, and about 3% of people over age 75 have it. About 200,000 new cases of epilepsy are diagnosed each year.

Most seizures are benign, but a seizure that lasts a long time can lead to status epilepticus, a life-threatening condition characterized by continuous seizures, sustained loss of consciousness, and respiratory distress. Non-convulsive epilepsy can impair physical coordination, vision, and other senses. Undiagnosed seizures can lead to conditions that are more serious and more difficult to manage.

Types of Seizures

Generalized epileptic seizures occur when electrical abnormalities occur throughout the brain. A partial seizure does not involve the entire brain. The area in which the seizure begins is called the epileptic focus. Many seizures stay localized, but some spread to other parts of the brain and cause a generalized seizure. Some people who have epilepsy have more than one type of seizure.

Seizures which involve areas of the brain necessary for motor control can cause parts of the body to jerk repeatedly. This type of seizure can last seconds or minutes or, rarely, more than an hour. Seizures that last more than a few minutes can cause serious long-term disability and even death. Sensory seizures begin with numbness or tingling in one area. The sensation may move along one side of the body or the back before subsiding.

Visual seizures, which affect the area of the brain that controls sight, cause people to see things that are not there. Auditory seizures affect the part of the brain that controls hearing and may cause the individual to imagine voices, music, or other sounds. Other types of seizures can cause confusion, upset stomach, or emotional distress.

Generalized Seizures. A generalized tonic-clonic (grand mal) seizure begins with a loud cry before the person having the seizure loses consciousness and falls to the ground. The muscles become rigid for about 30 seconds during the tonic phase of the seizure and alternately contract and relax during the clonic phase, which lasts 30–60 seconds. The skin sometimes acquires a bluish tint and the person may bite his tongue, lose bowel or bladder control, or have trouble breathing.

A grand mal seizure usually last one to two minutes, and the person may be confused or have trouble talking when consciousness is regained (postictal state). The individual may complain of head or muscle aches, weakness in the arms or legs, or be extremely drowsy or fatigued.

A primary generalized seizure occurs when electrical discharges begin in both halves (hemispheres) of the brain at the same time. Primary generalized seizures are more likely to be major motor attacks than to be absence seizures.

Particular Movements Characterize the Different Seizures

Absence Seizures. Absence (petit mal) seizures generally begin between the ages of 5 and 15. The seizures usually begin with a brief loss of consciousness and last between 2 and 3 seconds. Sometimes the episodes may last up to 30 seconds. An individual having a petit mal seizure becomes very quiet and may blink or stare blankly and may exhibit facial twitching, eye rolling, or lip movement. When it ends, the individual who had the seizure resumes whatever he or she was doing before the seizure began. The individual will not remember the seizure and may not realize that anything unusual has happened. Untreated, petit mal seizures can recur as many as 100 times a day and may progress to grand mal seizures.

Myoclonic Seizures. Myoclonic seizures are characterized by brief, involuntary spasms of the tongue or muscles of the face, arms, or legs. Myoclonic seizures are most apt to occur when waking after a night's sleep. These seizures do not generally cause loss of consciousness.

A Jacksonian seizure is a partial seizure characterized by tingling, stiffening, or jerking of an arm or leg. Loss of consciousness is rare. The seizure may progress in characteristic fashion along the limb.

Limp posture and a brief period of unconsciousness are features of atonic seizures, which occur in young children. Atonic seizures, which cause the child to fall, also are called drop attacks.

Partial Seizures. Simple partial seizures do not spread from the focal area where they arise. Symptoms are determined by the part of the brain affected. The individual usually remains conscious during the seizure and may be able to describe it later.

A distinctive smell, taste, or other unusual sensation (aura) may signal the start of a complex partial seizure. These seizures start as simple partial seizures, but move beyond the focal area and cause loss of consciousness. Complex partial seizures can become major motor seizures. Although a person having a complex partial seizure may not seem to be unconscious, he or she does not know what is happening and may behave strangely or inappropriately. The individual will not remember the seizure, and may seem confused or intoxicated for a few minutes after it ends.

FAST FACT

Fifty percent of those who have a seizure will have another. More than 70 percent of those who have two seizure will have another.

Causes of Epilepsy

The origin of 50–70% of all cases of epilepsy is unknown. Epilepsy sometimes is the result of trauma at birth. Such causes include insufficient oxygen to the brain; head injury; heavy bleeding or incompatibility between a woman's blood and the blood of her newborn baby; and infection immediately before, after, or at the time of birth.

Other causes of epilepsy include:

- head trauma resulting from a car accident, gunshot wound, or other injury
- alcoholism
- brain abscess or inflammation of membranes covering the brain or spinal cord
- phenylketonuria (PKU, a disease that is present at birth, often is characterized by seizures, and can result in mental retardation) and other inherited disorders
- infectious diseases like measles, mumps, and diphtheria
- degenerative disease
- lead poisoning, mercury poisoning, carbon monoxide poisoning, or ingestion of some other poisonous substance
- genetic factors

Status epilepticus, a condition in which a person suffers from continuous seizures and may have trouble breathing, can be caused by:

- suddenly discontinuing anti-seizure medication
- hypoxic or metabolic encephalopathy (brain disease resulting from lack of oxygen or malfunctioning of other physical or chemical processes)
- acute head injury
- blood infection caused by inflammation of the brain or the membranes that cover it

Diagnosing Epilepsy

Personal and family medical history, description of seizure activity, and physical and neurological examinations help primary care physicians, neurologists, and epileptologists diagnose this disorder. Doctors rule out conditions that cause symptoms that resemble epilepsy, including small strokes (transient ischemic attacks, or TIAs), fainting (syncope), pseudoseizures, and sleep attacks (narcolepsy). It is often helpful for a family member or other person present during the seizure to describe the event to the physician, as the individual who had the seizure may not remember it.

Neuropsychological testing can uncover any learning or memory problems that may be related to the seizure or seizures. Neuroimaging provides views of brain areas involved in seizure activity. The electroencephalogram (EEG) is the main test used to diagnose epilepsy. EEGs use electrodes placed on or within the skull to record the brain's electrical activity and pinpoint the exact location of abnormal discharges.

The patient may be asked to remain motionless during a short-term EEG or to go about his normal activities during extended monitoring. Some patients are deprived of sleep or exposed to seizure triggers, such as rapid, deep breathing (hyperventilation) or flashing lights (photic stimulation). In some cases, people may be hospitalized for EEG monitoring that can last as long as two weeks. Video EEGs also document what the patient was doing when the seizure occurred and how the seizure changed his or her behavior.

Other techniques used to diagnose epilepsy include:

• Magnetic resonance imaging (MRI), which provides clear, detailed images of the brain. Functional MRI (fMRI), performed while the patient does various tasks, can measure shifts in electrical intensity and blood flow and indicate which brain region each activity affects.

• Positron emission tomography (PET) and single photon emission tomography (SPECT) monitor blood flow and chemical activity in the brain area being tested. PET and SPECT are very effective in locating the brain region where metabolic changes take place between seizures.

Drug Therapy for Patients with Epilepsy

The goal of epilepsy treatment is to eliminate seizures or make the symptoms less frequent and less severe. Long-term anticonvulsant drug therapy is the most common form of epilepsy treatment.

A combination of drugs may be needed to control some symptoms, but most patients who have epilepsy take one of the following medications:

• Dilantin (phenytoin)
• Tegretol (carbamazepine)
• Barbita (phenobarbital)
• Mysoline (primidone)
• Depakene (valproic acid, sodium valproate)
• Klonopin (clonazepam)
• Zarontin (ethosuximide).

Dilantin, Tegretol, Barbita, and Mysoline are frequently used to manage or control generalized tonic-clonic and complex partial seizures. Depakene, Klonopin, and Zarontin are often prescribed for patients who have absence seizures.

Neurontin (gabapentin), Lamictal (lamotrigine), and topiramate (Topamax) are among the medications more recently approved in the United States to treat adults who have partial seizures or partial and grand mal seizures. Another new medication called Levetiracetam (Keppra) has been approved and shows particularly good results in reducing partial seizures among elderly patients with few side effects. This is important, because elderly patients often have other conditions and must take other

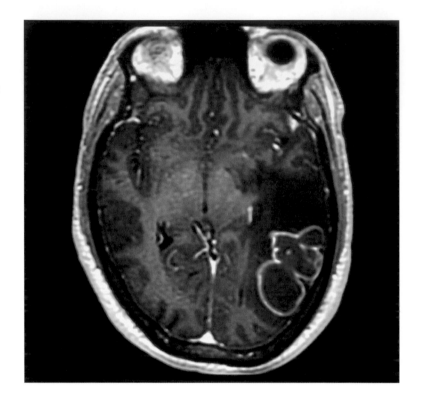

The red area shown on this MRI of the human brain highlights a cerebral abscess responsible for epileptic seizures. (BSIP/Photo Researchers, Inc.)

medications that might interact with seizure medications. Available medications frequently change, and the physician will determine the best treatment for an individual patient. It is believed that monotherapy, or using just one medication rather than a combination, may work better for most patients. The less complicated the treatment, the more likely the patient will comply and better manage the seizure disorder.

Even an individual whose seizures are well controlled should have regular blood tests to measure levels of anti-seizure medication in his or her system and to check to see if the medication is causing any changes in the blood or liver. A doctor should be notified if any signs of drug toxicity appear, including uncontrolled eye movements; sluggishness, dizziness, or hyperactivity; inability to see clearly or speak distinctly; nausea or vomiting; or sleep problems.

Status epilepticus requires emergency treatment, usually with Valium (or Ativan), Dilantin, or Barbita. An intravenous dextrose (sugar) solution is given to patients whose condition is due to low blood sugar, and a vitamin B1 [thiamine] preparation is administered intravenously when status epilepticus results from chronic alcohol withdrawal. Because dextrose and thiamine are essentially harmless and because delay in treatment can be disastrous, these medications are given routinely, as it is usually difficult to obtain an adequate history from a patient suffering from status epilepticus.

Intractable seizures are seizures that cannot be controlled with medication or without sedation or other unacceptable side effects. Surgery may be used to eliminate or control intractable seizures.

Surgery May Help

Surgery can be used to treat patients whose intractable seizures stem from small focal lesions that can be removed without endangering the patient, changing the patient's personality, dulling the patient's senses, or reducing the patient's ability to function.

Each year, as many as 5,000 new patients may become suitable candidates for surgery, which most often is performed at a comprehensive epilepsy center. Potential surgical candidates include patients with:

- partial seizures and secondarily generalized seizures (attacks that begin in one area and spread to both sides of the brain)
- seizures and childhood paralysis on one side of the body (hemiplegia)
- complex partial seizures originating in the temporal lobe (the part of the brain associated with speech, hearing, and smell) or other focal seizures. (However, the risk of surgery involving the speech centers is that the patient will lose speech function.)

- Generalized myoclonic seizures or generalized seizures featuring temporary paralysis (akinetic) or loss of muscle tone (atonal)

A physical examination is conducted to verify that a patient's seizures are caused by epilepsy. Surgery is not used to treat patients with severe psychiatric disturbances or medical problems that raise risk factors to unacceptable levels.

Surgery is never indicated unless:

- the best available anti-seizure medications have failed to control the patient's symptoms satisfactorily
- the origin of the patient's seizures has been precisely located
- there is good reason to believe that surgery will significantly improve the patient's health and quality of life.

Every patient considering epilepsy surgery is carefully evaluated by one or more neurologists, neurosurgeons, neuropsychologists, and/or social workers. A psychiatrist, chaplain, or other spiritual advisor may help the patient and his family cope with the stress that occurs during and after the selection process.

Types of Surgery

Surgical techniques used to treat intractable epilepsy include:

- *Lesionectomy*. Removing the lesion (diseased brain tissue) and some surrounding brain tissue is very effective in controlling seizures. Lesionectomy is generally more successful than surgery performed on individuals whose seizures are not caused by clearly defined lesions. Removing only part of the lesion lessens the effectiveness of the procedure.

- *Temporal resections.* Removing part of the temporal lobe and the part of the brain associated with feelings, memory, and emotions (the hippocampus) provides good or excellent seizure control in 75–80% of properly selected patients with appropriate types of temporal lobe epilepsy. Some patients experience post-operative speech and memory problems.
- *Extra-temporal resection.* This procedure involves removing some or all of the frontal lobe, the part of the brain directly behind the forehead. The frontal lobe helps regulate movement, planning, judgment, and personality. Special care must be taken to prevent post-operative problems with movement and speech. Extra-temporal resection is most successful in patients whose seizures are not widespread.
- *Hemispherectomy.* This method of removing brain tissue is restricted to patients with severe epilepsy and abnormal discharges that often extend from one side of the brain to the other. Hemispherectomies most often are performed on infants or young children who have had an extensive brain disease or disorder since birth or from a very young age.
- *Corpus callosotomy.* This procedure, an alternative to hemispherectomy in patients with congenital hemiplegia, removes some or all of the white matter that separates the two halves of the brain. Corpus callosotomy is performed almost exclusively on children who are frequently injured during falls caused by seizures. If removing two-thirds of the corpus callosum does not produce lasting improvement in the patient's condition, the remaining one-third will be removed during another operation.
- *Multiple subpial transection.* This procedure is used to control the spread of seizures that originate in or affect the "eloquent" cortex, the area of the brain responsible for complex thought and reasoning.

The Ketogenic Diet

A special high-fat, low-protein, low-carbohydrate diet sometimes is used to treat patients whose severe seizures have not responded to other treatment. Calculated according to age, height, and weight, the ketogenic diet induces mild starvation and dehydration. This forces the body to create an excessive supply of ketones, natural chemicals with seizure-suppressing properties.

The goal of this controversial approach is to maintain or improve seizure control while reducing medication. The ketogenic diet works best with children between the ages of one and 10. It is introduced over a period of several days, and most children are hospitalized during the early stages of treatment.

If a child following this diet remains seizure-free for at least six months, increased amounts of carbohydrates and protein gradually are added. If the child shows no improvement after three months, the diet is gradually discontinued.

Introduced in the 1920s, the ketogenic diet has had limited, short-term success in controlling seizure activity. Its use exposes patients to such potentially harmful side effects as:

- staphylococcal infections
- stunted or delayed growth
- low blood sugar (hypoglycemia)
- excess fat in the blood (hyperlipidemia)
- disease resulting from calcium deposits in the urinary tract (urolithiasis)
- disease of the optic nerve (optic neuropathy)

Nerve Stimulation and First Aid

The United States Food and Drug Administration (FDA) has approved the use of vagus nerve stimulation (VNS) in patients over the age of 16 who have intractable partial seizures. This non-surgical procedure uses a pacemaker-like device implanted under the skin in the upper left chest,

Functions of the Brain

Commonly, seizures will originate in a particular brain area, affecting the functions for which that area is responsible. Auras, or the warning signs that come before a seizure, may also be linked to the brain section's unique functions.

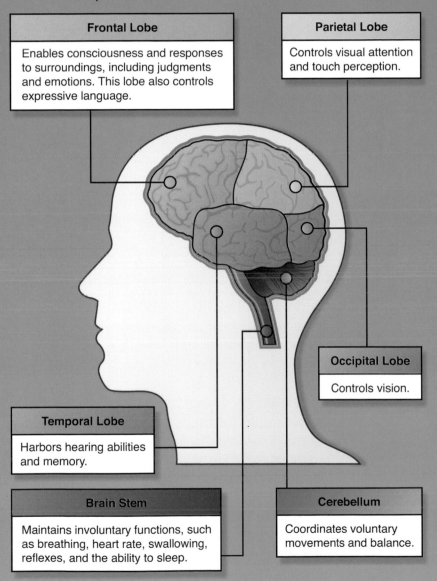

Frontal Lobe

Enables consciousness and responses to surroundings, including judgments and emotions. This lobe also controls expressive language.

Parietal Lobe

Controls visual attention and touch perception.

Occipital Lobe

Controls vision.

Temporal Lobe

Harbors hearing abilities and memory.

Brain Stem

Maintains involuntary functions, such as breathing, heart rate, swallowing, reflexes, and the ability to sleep.

Cerebellum

Coordinates voluntary movements and balance.

Taken from: James Knupp, "Mysteries of the Human Brain," *The Human Brain*, 2005.
www.wright.edu/academics/honors/institute/brain/mysteries.html.

to provide intermittent stimulation to the vagus nerve. Stretching from the side of the neck into the brain, the vagus nerve affects swallowing, speech, breathing, and many other functions, and VNS may prevent or shorten some seizures. Approximately 80% of patients experience fewer seizures after the procedure. Individuals having undergone this procedure may experience side effects such as dizziness, memory loss, weight gain, and slurred speech.

A person having a seizure should not be restrained, but sharp or dangerous objects should be moved out of reach. Anyone having a complex partial seizure may be warned away from danger by someone calling his or her name in a clear, calm voice.

A person having a grand mal seizure should be helped to lie down. Tight clothing should be loosened. A soft, flat object like a towel or the palm of a hand should be placed under the person's head. Forcing objects into the mouth of someone having a grand mal seizure could cause injuries or breathing problems, and the individual trying to help may be injured if the jaw clenches shut. The individual having the seizure should be turned on his or her side if consciousness has been lost. This will ensure the individual is able to breathe. After a grand mal seizure has ended, the person who had the seizure should be calmly told what has happened and reminded of where he or she is.

Alternative Treatments

Stress increases seizure activity in 30% of people who have epilepsy. Relaxation techniques can provide some sense of control over the disorder, but they should never be used instead of anti-seizure medication or used without the approval of the patient's doctor. Yoga, meditation, and favorite pastimes help some people relax and manage stress more successfully. Biofeedback [a learning technique that helps individuals influence automatic body functions] can teach adults and older adolescents how to recognize an aura and what to do to stop its spread. Children under

14 are not usually able to understand and apply principles of biofeedback. Acupuncture treatments (acupuncture needles inserted for a few minutes or left in place for as long as 30 minutes) make some people feel pleasantly relaxed. Acupressure can have the same effect on children or on adults who dislike needles.

Aromatherapy involves mixing aromatic plant oils into water or other oils and massaging them into the skin or using a special burner to waft their fragrance throughout the room. Aromatherapy oils affect the body and the brain, and undiluted oils should never be applied directly to the skin. Ylang ylang, chamomile, or lavender can create a soothing mood. People who have epilepsy should not use rosemary, hyssop, sage or sweet fennel, which seem to make the brain more alert.

Dietary changes that emphasize whole foods and eliminate processed foods may be helpful. Homeopathic therapy also can work for people with seizures, especially constitutional homeopathic treatment that acts at the deepest levels to address the needs of the individual person.

Prognosis for Epilepsy

People who have epilepsy have a higher-than-average rate of suicide; sudden, unexplained death; and drowning and other accidental fatalities.

Benign focal epilepsy of childhood and some absence seizures may disappear in time, but remission is unlikely if seizures occur several times a day, several times in a 48-hour period, or more frequently than in the past.

Seizures that occur repeatedly over time and always involve the same symptoms are called stereotypic seizures. The probability that stereotypic seizures will abate is poor.

About 85% of all seizure disorders can be partially or completely controlled if the patient takes anti-seizure medication according to directions, avoids seizure-inducing sights, sounds, and other triggers, gets enough sleep, and eats regular, balanced meals.

Anyone who has epilepsy should wear a bracelet or necklace identifying the seizure disorder and listing the medication that he or she takes.

Preventive Measures

Eating properly, getting enough sleep, and controlling stress and fevers can help prevent seizures. A person who has epilepsy should be careful not to hyperventilate. A person who experiences an aura should find a safe place to lie down and stay there until the seizure passes. Anticonvulsant medications should not be stopped suddenly and, if other medications are prescribed or discontinued, the doctor treating the seizures should be notified. In some conditions, such as severe head injury, brain surgery, or subarachnoid hemorrhage, anticonvulsant medications may be given to the patient to prevent seizures.

The Causes of Epilepsy

National Institute of Neurological Disorders and Stroke

This essay, from a research report by the National Institute of Neurological Disorders and Stroke (NINDS), examines some of the many possible causes of epilepsy. Anything that disrupts normal neuronal activity in the brain can trigger recurring seizures, the prominent symptom of epilepsy. Abnormal nerve connections, chemical imbalances, and genetic factors can all contribute to epilepsy, the authors point out. Epilepsy may also develop because of brain damage resulting from other illnesses (such as heart disease, brain tumors, and Alzheimer's, among others), head injuries, poisoning, or developmental deficiencies. Within the U.S. Department of Health and Human Services, NINDS is an arm of the National Institutes of Health, located in Bethesda, Maryland.

Epilepsy is a brain disorder in which clusters of nerve cells, or neurons, in the brain sometimes signal abnormally. Neurons normally generate electrochemical impulses that act on other neurons,

SOURCE: "Seizures and Epilepsy: Hope Through Research," National Institute of Neurological Disorders and Stroke (NINDS), May, 2004. Reproduced by permission.

glands, and muscles to produce human thoughts, feelings, and actions. In epilepsy, the normal pattern of neuronal activity becomes disturbed, causing strange sensations, emotions, and behavior, or sometimes *convulsions*, muscle spasms, and loss of consciousness. During a seizure, neurons may fire as many as 500 times a second, much faster than normal. In some people, this happens only occasionally; for others, it may happen up to hundreds of times a day.

More than 2 million people in the United States—about 1 in 100—have experienced an unprovoked seizure or been diagnosed with epilepsy. For about 80 percent of those diagnosed with epilepsy, seizures can be controlled with modern medicines and surgical techniques. However, about 25 to 30 percent of people with epilepsy will continue to experience seizures even with the best available treatment. Doctors call this situation *intractable* epilepsy. Having a seizure does not necessarily mean that a person has epilepsy. Only when a person has had two or more seizures is he or she considered to have epilepsy.

Epilepsy is not contagious and is not caused by mental illness or mental retardation. Some people with mental retardation may experience seizures, but seizures do not necessarily mean the person has or will develop mental impairment. Many people with epilepsy have normal or above-average intelligence. Famous people who are known or rumored to have had epilepsy include the Russian writer [Fyodor] Dostoyevsky, the philosopher Socrates, the military general Napoleon [Bonaparte], and the inventor of dynamite, Alfred Nobel, who established the Nobel Prize. Several Olympic medalists and other athletes also have had epilepsy. Seizures sometimes do cause brain damage, particularly if they are severe. However, most seizures do not seem to have a detrimental effect on the brain. Any changes that do occur are usually subtle, and it is often unclear whether these changes are caused by the seizures themselves or by the underlying problem that caused the seizures.

Epilepsy Risk in Special Populations

The basic, underlying risk of developing epilepsy is about 1 percent. Individuals in certain populations are at higher risk. For example, it is estimated that epilepsy can be expected to develop in:

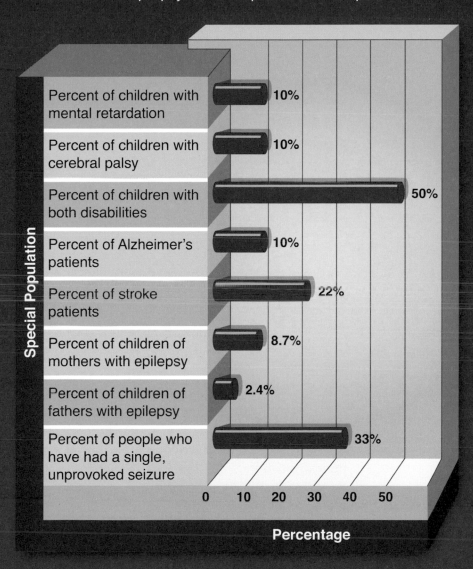

Taken from: Epilepsy Foundation, "About Epilepsy: Epilepsy and Seizure Statistics." www.epilepsyfoundation.org.

While epilepsy cannot currently be cured, for some people it does eventually go away. One study found that children with *idiopathic epilepsy*, or epilepsy with an unknown cause, had a 68 to 92 percent chance of becoming seizure-free by 20 years after their diagnosis. The odds of becoming seizure-free are not as good for adults or for children with severe epilepsy syndromes, but it is nonetheless possible that seizures may decrease or even stop over time. This is more likely if the epilepsy has been well-controlled by medication or if the person has had epilepsy surgery.

What Causes Epilepsy?

Epilepsy is a disorder with many possible causes. Anything that disturbs the normal pattern of neuron activity—from illness to brain damage to abnormal brain development—can lead to seizures.

Epilepsy may develop because of an abnormality in brain wiring, an imbalance of nerve signaling chemicals called *neurotransmitters*, or some combination of these factors. Researchers believe that some people with epilepsy have an abnormally high level of *excitatory neurotransmitters* that increase neuronal activity, while others have an abnormally low level of *inhibitory neurotransmitters* that decrease neuronal activity in the brain. Either situation can result in too much neuronal activity and cause epilepsy. One of the most-studied neurotransmitters that plays a role in epilepsy is *GABA*, or gamma-aminobutyric acid, which is an inhibitory neurotransmitter. Research on GABA has led to drugs that alter the amount of this neurotransmitter in the brain or change how the brain responds to it. Researchers also are studying excitatory neurotransmitters such as glutamate.

In some cases, the brain's attempts to repair itself after a head injury, stroke, or other problem may inadvertently generate abnormal nerve connections that lead to epilep-

> **FAST FACT**
>
> No cause is apparent in 70 percent of new cases of epilepsy.

sy. Abnormalities in brain wiring that occur during brain development also may disturb neuronal activity and lead to epilepsy.

Research has shown that the cell membrane that surrounds each neuron plays an important role in epilepsy. Cell membranes are crucial for a neuron to generate electrical impulses. For this reason, researchers are studying details of the membrane structure, how molecules move in and out of membranes, and how the cell nourishes and repairs the membrane. A disruption in any of these processes may lead to epilepsy. Studies in animals have shown that, because the brain continually adapts to changes in stimuli, a small change in neuronal activity, if repeated, may eventually lead to full-blown epilepsy. Researchers are investigating whether this phenomenon, called *kindling*, may also occur in humans.

In some cases, epilepsy may result from changes in non-neuronal brain cells called glia. These cells regulate concentrations of chemicals in the brain that can affect neuronal signaling.

About half of all seizures have no known cause. However, in other cases, the seizures are clearly linked to infection, trauma, or other identifiable problems.

Genetic Factors Are Significant in Some Cases

Research suggests that genetic abnormalities may be some of the most important factors contributing to epilepsy. Some types of epilepsy have been traced to an abnormality in a specific gene. Many other types of epilepsy tend to run in families, which suggests that genes influence epilepsy. Some researchers estimate that more than 500 genes could play a role in this disorder. However, it is increasingly clear that, for many forms of epilepsy, genetic abnormalities play only a partial role, perhaps by increasing a person's susceptibility to seizures that are triggered by an environmental factor.

Several types of epilepsy have now been linked to defective genes for *ion channels*, the "gates" that control the flow of ions in and out of cells and regulate neuron signaling. Another gene, which is missing in people with *progressive myoclonus epilepsy*, codes for a protein called cystatin B. This protein regulates enzymes that break down other proteins. Another gene, which is altered in a severe form of epilepsy called *LaFora's disease*, has been linked to a gene that helps to break down carbohydrates.

While abnormal genes sometimes cause epilepsy, they also may influence the disorder in subtler ways. For example, one study showed that many people with epilepsy have an abnormally active version of a gene that increases resistance to drugs. This may help explain why anticonvulsant drugs do not work for some people. Genes also may control other aspects of the body's response to medications and each person's susceptibility to seizures, or *seizure threshold*. Abnormalities in the genes that control neuronal migration—a critical step in brain development—can lead to areas of misplaced or abnormally formed neurons, or *dysplasia*, in the brain that can cause epilepsy. In some cases, genes may contribute to development of epilepsy even in people with no family history of the disorder. These people may have a newly developed abnormality, or *mutation*, in an epilepsy-related gene.

The Results of Other Disorders and Injuries

In many cases, epilepsy develops as a result of brain damage from other disorders. For example, brain tumors, alcoholism, and Alzheimer's disease frequently lead to epilepsy because they alter the normal workings of the brain. Strokes, heart attacks, and other conditions that deprive the brain of oxygen also can cause epilepsy in some cases. About 32 percent of all cases of newly developed epilepsy in elderly people appears to be due to

Nearly half of all epileptic seizures have no known cause, but the rest are linked to head injury, infection, and other identifiable problems. (© **Angela Hampton Picture Library/ Alamy**)

cerebrovascular disease, which reduces the supply of oxygen to brain cells. Meningitis, AIDS, viral encephalitis, and other infectious diseases can lead to epilepsy, as can hydrocephalus—a condition in which excess fluid builds up in the brain. Epilepsy also can result from intolerance to wheat gluten (also known as *celiac disease*), or from a parasitic infection of the brain called *neurocysticercosis*. Seizures may stop once these disorders are treated successfully. However, the odds of becoming seizure-free after the primary disorder is treated are uncertain and vary depending on the type of disorder, the brain region that is affected, and how much brain damage occurred prior to treatment.

Epilepsy is associated with a variety of developmental and metabolic disorders, including cerebral palsy, neurofibromatosis, pyruvate dependency, tuberous sclerosis, Landau-Kleffner syndrome, and autism. Epilepsy is just one of a set of symptoms commonly found in people with these disorders.

In some cases, head injury can lead to seizures or epilepsy. Safety measures such as wearing seat belts in cars and using helmets when riding a motorcycle or playing competitive sports can protect people from epilepsy and other problems that result from head injury.

The developing brain is susceptible to many kinds of injury. Maternal infections, poor nutrition, and oxygen deficiencies are just some of the conditions that may take a toll on the brain of a developing baby. These conditions may lead to cerebral palsy, which often is associated with epilepsy, or they may cause epilepsy that is unrelated to any other disorders. About 20 percent of seizures in children are due to cerebral palsy or other neurological abnormalities. Abnormalities in genes that control development also may contribute to epilepsy. Advanced brain imaging has revealed that some cases of epilepsy that occur with no obvious cause may be associated with areas of dysplasia in the brain that probably develop before birth.

Seizures can result from exposure to lead, carbon monoxide, and many other poisons. They also can result from exposure to street drugs and from overdoses of antidepressants and other medications.

Seizures are often triggered by factors such as lack of sleep, alcohol consumption, stress, or hormonal changes associated with the menstrual cycle. These *seizure triggers* do not cause epilepsy but can provoke first seizures or cause breakthrough seizures in people who otherwise experience good seizure control with their medication. Sleep deprivation in particular is a universal and powerful trigger of seizures. For this reason, people with epilepsy should make sure to get enough sleep and should try to stay on a regular sleep schedule as much as possible. For some people, light flashing at a certain speed or the flicker of a computer monitor can trigger a seizure; this problem is called *photosensitive epilepsy*. Smoking cigarettes also can trigger seizures. The nicotine in cigarettes acts on receptors for the excitatory neurotransmitter acetylcholine in the brain, which increases neuronal firing. Seizures are not triggered by sexual activity except in very rare instances.

Myths and Facts About Epilepsy

Orrin Devinsky

In the past, epilepsy was often considered to be a curse from the gods, a sign of witchcraft, or a contagious disease, notes Orrin Devinsky in the following selection. Since the early twentieth century, developments in brain and neurological research have led to a greater understanding of this disorder, but some misconceptions remain. For example, the popular notions that people with epilepsy are intellectually inferior, violent, or mentally ill are all untrue. Epilepsy is not necessarily inherited, nor is it usually a lifelong disorder, the author asserts. While some forms of epilepsy may be more difficult to control than others, the majority of people with this disorder can lead happy, successful lives. Devinsky is a physician and director of the New York University Epilepsy Center.

Epilepsy has afflicted human beings since the dawn of our species and has been recognized since the earliest medical writings. We now understand that epilepsy (commonly called 'the epilepsies') is a group of disorders that occurs as a result of seizures that tempo-

SOURCE: Orrin Devinsky, "Facts & Myths," Epilepsy.com, June, 2006. Copyright © 2008 Epilepsy.com. Reproduced by permission.

rarily impair brain function. Epilepsy is not a 'one size fits all problem'. It can look, feel and act differently in different people. It is much more common than previously thought and is one of the more common neurological problems affecting people of all ages. Few medical conditions have attracted so much attention and generated so much controversy. Throughout history, people with epilepsy and their families have suffered unfairly because of the ignorance of others. Fortunately, the stigma and fear generated by the words "seizures" and "epilepsy" have decreased during the past century, and most people with epilepsy now lead normal lives.

From Falsehood to Understanding

The Greek physician Hippocrates wrote the first book on epilepsy, titled *On the Sacred Disease,* around 400 B.C. Hippocrates recognized that epilepsy was a brain disorder, and he spoke out against the ideas that seizures were a curse from the gods and that people with epilepsy held the power of prophecy.

Sadly, false ideas die slowly, and for centuries epilepsy was considered a curse of the gods, or worse. For example, a 1494 handbook on witch-hunting, *Malleus Maleficarum*, written by two Dominican friars, said that one of the ways of identifying a witch was by the presence of seizures. This book guided a wave of persecution and torture, which caused the deaths of up to 100,000 women thought to be witches.

Misunderstanding continued for many more years. In the early 19th century, people who had severe epilepsy and people with psychiatric disorders were cared for in asylums, but the two groups were kept separated because seizures were thought to be contagious. In the early 1900s, some U.S. states had laws forbidding people with epilepsy to marry or become parents, and some states permitted sterilization.

The modern medical era of epilepsy began in the mid-1800s, under the leadership of three English neurologists: Russell Reynolds, John Hughlings Jackson, and Sir William Richard Gowers. Still standing today is Hughlings Jackson's definition of a seizure as "an occasional, an excessive, and a disorderly discharge of nerve tissue on muscles." Hughlings Jackson also pointed out that seizures could alter consciousness, sensation, and behavior.

The past century has brought an explosion of knowledge about the functions of the brain and about epilepsy. Epilepsy research continues at a vigorous pace, with investigations ranging from how microscopic particles and channels in the cell trigger seizures, to the development of new seizure medicines, and to a better understanding of how epilepsy affects social and intellectual development.

Misleading Terms

People with epilepsy are not "epileptics." The word "epileptic" should not be used to describe someone who has epilepsy, as it defines a person by one trait or problem. A label is powerful and can create a limiting and negative stereotype. It is better to refer to someone as "a person with epilepsy" or to a group of people as "people with epilepsy."

A seizure disorder is epilepsy. Because some people fear the word "epilepsy," they use the term "seizure disorder" in an attempt to separate themselves from any association with it. However the term seizure disorder means the same thing as epilepsy. A person has epilepsy or a seizure disorder if he or she has had two or more seizures that "come out of the blue" and are not provoked—even if the problem first develops in adulthood or is known to be caused by something like a severe head injury or a tumor.

People with epilepsy are seldom brain-damaged. Epilepsy is a disorder of brain and nerve-cell function that may or may not be associated with damage to brain structures. Brain *function* can be temporarily disturbed by many things, such as extreme fatigue; the use of sleeping pills, sedatives, or general anesthesia; or high fever or serious illness. "Brain damage" implies that something is permanently wrong with the brain's structure. This kind of damage may occur with severe head injury, cerebral palsy, or stroke, or it may occur long before birth, with malformation or infection. Injuries to the brain are the cause of seizures in some people with epilepsy, but by no means all of them.

Brain injuries range from undetectable to disabling. Although brain cells usually do not regenerate, most people can make substantial recoveries. Brain damage, like epilepsy, carries a stigma, and some people may unjustly consider brain-injured patients "incompetent."

> ## FAST FACT
>
> Epilepsy can affect anyone at any age. However, the disease most often begins either in childhood or after the age of sixty.

People with epilepsy are not usually cognitively challenged. People with epilepsy usually are not intellectually challenged. Many people mistakenly believe that people with epilepsy are also intellectually or developmentally challenged. In the large majority of situations, this is not true. Like any other group of people, people with epilepsy have different intellectual abilities. Some are brilliant and some score below average on intelligence tests, but most are somewhere in the middle. They have normal intelligence and lead productive lives. Some people, however, may have epilepsy associated with brain injuries that may cause other neurological difficulties that affect their thinking, remembering, or other cognitive abilities. The cognitive problems may be the only problem in most people. Less frequently, some people have other developmental problems that can affect the way they function and live.

Epilepsy Is Often Misunderstood

People with epilepsy are not violent or crazy. The belief that people with epilepsy are violent is an unfortunate image that is both wrong and destructive. People with epilepsy have no greater tendency toward severe irritability and aggressive behaviors than do other people.

John H. Jackson was a nineteenth-century neurologist who pioneered epilepsy research and whose definition of a seizure still stands today. (Hulton Archive/Getty Images)

Many features of seizures and their immediate after-effects can be easily misunderstood as "crazy" or "violent" behavior. Unfortunately, police officers and even medical personnel may confuse seizure-related behaviors with other problems. However, these behaviors merely represent semiconscious or confused actions resulting from the seizure. During seizures, some people may not respond to questions, may speak gibberish, undress, repeat a word or phrase, crumple important papers, or may appear frightened and scream. Some are confused immediately after a seizure, and if they are restrained or prevented from moving about, they can become agitated and combative. Some people are able to respond to questions and carry on a conversation fairly well, but several hours later they cannot remember the conversation at all.

People with epilepsy are not mentally ill. Epilepsy is not the same as mental illness and in fact, the majority of people with seizures do not develop mental health problems. Yet recent research is showing that problems with mood, such as anxiety and depression, may be seen more frequently than previously thought. The causes are not always known. In some people, the cause and location of the seizures may affect certain brain areas and contribute to mood problems. In others, side effects of treatments and the challenges of living with epilepsy may affect a person's feelings and behavior. If these problems occur, a variety of treatments are available.

Seizures do not cause brain damage. Single tonic-clonic seizures lasting less than 5–10 minutes are not known to cause brain damage or injury. However, there is evidence that more frequent and more prolonged tonic-clonic seizures may in some patients injure the brain. Prolonged or repetitive complex partial seizures (a type of seizure that occurs in clusters without an intervening return of consciousness) also can potentially cause long-lasting impairment of brain function.

Some people have difficulty with memory and other intellectual functions after a seizure. These problems may be caused by the aftereffects of the seizure on the brain, by the effects of seizure medicines, or both. Usually, however, these problems do not mean that the brain has been damaged by the seizure. There may be a cumulative, negative effect of many tonic-clonic or complex partial seizures on brain function, but this effect appears to be rare.

Epilepsy is not necessarily inherited. Most cases of epilepsy are not inherited, although some types are genetically transmitted (that is, passed on through the family).

Most of these types are easily controlled with seizure medicines.

Epilepsy Is Usually Manageable

Epilepsy is not a life-long disorder. Generally, people with epilepsy have seizures and require medication for only a small portion of their lives. About 60% of people who develop seizures have epilepsy that can be easily controlled and is likely to remit or go away. However, about 25% may develop difficult to control seizures and likely will require lifelong treatment. More than half of childhood forms of epilepsy are outgrown by adulthood. With many forms of epilepsy in children and adults, when the person has been free of seizures for 1 to 3 years, medications can often be slowly withdrawn and discontinued under a doctor's supervision.

Epilepsy is not a curse. Epilepsy has nothing to do with curses, possession, or other supernatural processes, such as punishment for past sins. Like asthma, diabetes, and high blood pressure, epilepsy is a medical problem.

Epilepsy should not be a barrier to success. Epilepsy is perfectly compatible with a normal, happy, and full life. The person's quality of life, however, may be affected by the frequency and severity of the seizures, the effects of medications, reactions of onlookers to seizures, and other disorders that are often associated with or caused by epilepsy.

Some types of epilepsy are harder to control than others. Living successfully with epilepsy requires a positive outlook, a supportive environment, and good medical care. Coping with the reaction of other people to the disorder can be the most difficult part of living with epilepsy.

Acquiring a positive outlook may be easier said than done, especially for those who have grown up with insecurity and fear. Instilling a strong sense of self-esteem in children is important. Many children with long-term,

A Sampling of Famous People with Epilepsy

Artists & Writers	
Edgar Allan Poe	Lewis Carroll
Lord Byron	Fyodor Dostoyevsky
Charles Dickens	Agatha Christie
Vincent van Gogh	Truman Capote

Actors	
Richard Burton	Danny Glover
Margaux Hemingway	Michael Wilding

World Leaders	
Alexander the Great	Napoleon Bonaparte
Julius Caesar	

Composers	
George Frideric Handel	Niccolo Paganini
Peter Tchaikovsky	

Taken from: "Famous People with Epilepsy," December 15, 2006. www.epilepsy.com.

ongoing illnesses—not only epilepsy but also disorders such as asthma or diabetes—have low self-esteem. This may be caused in part by the reactions of others and in part by parental concern that fosters dependence and insecurity. Children develop strong self-esteem and independence through praise for their accomplishments and emphasis on their potential abilities.

Teens Should Be Involved in Managing Their Epilepsy

Patricia Osborne Shafer and Colleen DiIorio

The following selection offers an overview of some of the special dilemmas that teenagers with epilepsy must confront. The transition from childhood to adulthood is typically challenging, the authors point out—but a teen with epilepsy faces additional problems because seizures can interfere with one's physical, emotional, and social life. Dealing with stigma, developing confidence, accepting the support of friends and family, managing seizures, and maintaining emotional well-being require healthy communication between parents, care providers, and teens with epilepsy. The authors contend that a well-designed "team-centered" approach involving doctors, counselors, educators, various specialists, parents, and the teens themselves can empower youths as they learn to live successfully with epilepsy. Patricia Osborne Shafer is a specialty care nurse who also has epilepsy. Colleen DiIorio, who has written several articles on neuroscience nursing, is a public health professor at Emory University in Atlanta, Georgia.

SOURCE: Patricia Osborne Shafer and Colleen DiIorio, "Self-Management in Epilepsy Care: Putting Teens and Families in the Center," *Exceptional Parent Magazine,* June 2006. Copyright © 2006 EP Global Communications, Inc. Reproduced by permission.

Epilepsy is one of the most common chronic neurological problems in childhood and adolescence. Unfortunately, it is also one of the most misunderstood conditions. Epilepsy can interfere with the physical, emotional and social functioning of youth of all ages, particularly if seizures are uncontrolled. Teenagers living with epilepsy face unique challenges as they make the transition from childhood to adulthood and shift away from depending on others to learning how to take care of themselves. Treating seizures effectively and preventing unexpected consequences requires a collaborative effort between health care providers, caregivers, families, and the teenager with epilepsy. . . .

Epilepsy is simply the term used to describe recurring seizures that are not provoked or caused by a specific illness. For example, seizures that occur only with a fever are not considered a form of epilepsy. However, if a person later develops seizures that can occur without fevers, then that person would be considered to have a form of epilepsy. This term is often used interchangeably with seizure disorders. A seizure is a symptom of a neurological disorder and is the result of abnormal electrical activity in the brain that occurs suddenly and unpredictably, interfering with normal brain activity and causing a seizure to occur. During a seizure, behavioral changes occur, for example, altered awareness, thinking, talking, moving, feeling or perceptions. Exactly what happens depends on the area of brain affected. Generalized forms of seizures tend to predominate in childhood, yet partial seizures, or seizures beginning in one area of the brain, tend to increase in adolescence and early adult years.

Seizures can occur at any age, but epilepsy tends to start most often in children and older adults. There are over 300,000 youth aged 14 years or less in the United States with epilepsy. While some forms of epilepsy may be short-lived and easy to control with medications, approximately 25% of people who develop seizures will have seizures that are not controlled (also called refractory or intractable epilepsy). Research in recent years has suggested that epilepsy can become a much more serious disorder than commonly thought, with 40% of people continuing to have seizures after only the second medication tried. More than half of people with epilepsy may require medications for years, possibly throughout their life.

Problems Faced by Teens with Seizures

Seizures are not the only problem facing our adolescents. Physical, social and emotional problems can occur that affect a child's growth and development in critical ways, such as interfering with self-competence, physical function, peer relationships, independence, and school competence. These problems may occur for many reasons. Epilepsy can disrupt the way some of the brain cells function, while the frequency of seizures can affect this even more. The underlying cause of epilepsy and side effects of treatment may contribute to the problems that teens experience, as well as the challenges of coping with a chronic, unpredictable health problem. It is important to understand that epilepsy is not a "one size fits all" problem. Seizures and the associated problems can look and feel different from one person to the next. Some teens may have very few problems and manage well without additional help. For others, seizures may be only part of the picture. Other neurological problems may be present, or the seizure frequency or severity is such that specialized help from heath care professionals, families, schools, and community resources is needed. People of all ages with uncontrolled seizures tend to experience the greatest difficulties, yet psychosocial problems may occur even in youth with well-controlled epilepsy.

How do teens view epilepsy? A survey of 19,441 teens in the general population who did not have seizures showed that the majority of teens did not understand and were not familiar with epilepsy. Many misperceptions were found; 40% of respondents were not sure if

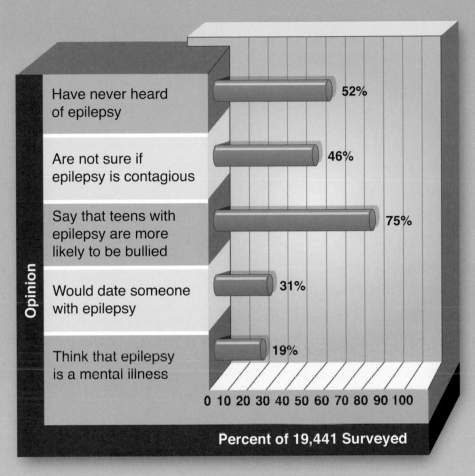

Teens' Opinions About Epilepsy

Opinion	Percent
Have never heard of epilepsy	52%
Are not sure if epilepsy is contagious	46%
Say that teens with epilepsy are more likely to be bullied	75%
Would date someone with epilepsy	31%
Think that epilepsy is a mental illness	19%

0 10 20 30 40 50 60 70 80 90 100

Percent of 19,441 Surveyed

Taken from: Joan Austin and Patricia Osborne Shafer, *Epilepsy Behavior*, 2002.

teens with seizures were dangerous and 75% believed that teens with epilepsy were more likely to be bullied or teased than other children. These plain facts highlight some of the social problems that teens may face as they learn to manage life with seizures.

Teen Voices

Another way to understand the teen experience is to read their stories. Teens from around the world have shared their experiences on Epilepsy.com, an online forum for the general public and people with epilepsy. The following are excerpts from teen stories posted on Epilepsy.com.

Teen #1, age 18: "My medication had loads of side effects: I felt sick, I put on weight and I felt so drowsy all the time, which affected my schoolwork, I would often just get home from school at about quarter to four, flop down on the sofa and just sleep until about seven o'clock. Of course, this ended up just making the problem worse because it meant I couldn't sleep at night, so when I got up in the morning I would have a tonic clonic seizure due to lack of sleep. . . . Can remember one time I had a tonic clonic seizure at school. . . . Most of the other children were staring round at me. Some looked shocked, others very frightened. Most of the children were OK about my seizure once they had calmed down, but some were scared to play with me at break time in case it happened again. There were times, though, that I knew I was 'different' to the other children and sometimes I felt singled out. I sometimes felt isolated, because I didn't know anybody else who had epilepsy who I could chat to about it. My school teacher, my family and most of my friends were very supportive towards me . . . but I feel that it is sometimes difficult for them to really understand what it is like if they haven't been through it themselves. . . . I have to think about my health and safety as well."

Teen #2, age 14: "I've been diagnosed with epilepsy for about 5 years. I think that I had it for more years, months, maybe days. I was an energetic girl. . . . I made everybody's day bright with just a simple hello. I wasn't afraid of nothing or to do anything. I had good grades in school—good enough to pass. Now I am a tired young girl, with little energy and grades that are barely passing."

Teen #3, age 17: "I was in 8th grade when I first found out I had epilepsy. It was in the middle of my science

FAST FACT

A 2006 survey found that most youths have misconceptions about epilepsy, including the notions that people with epilepsy are less honest, less popular, less fun, and less adept at sports than others.

class. Since that day, my life has never been the same. I love cars and I love being able to drive. If I forget just once to take my medicine, my parents take away my car for a week because they're scared I'll have a seizure. Most of the kids think that epilepsy is a joke, or a disease. They don't think it's really anything to worry about. They don't understand how hard it really is to cope with the idea that if I have a tonic-clonic seizure, I won't be able to dance again. It's hard to make them understand. They all think I get special treatment because I have epilepsy, but it's not true. I just wish I could make them understand."

Teen #4: "I remember just coming home from work, with a pounding headache, going for the computer to check my e-mail. However, my mind goes blank from there. The next thing I knew I was in an ambulance, with a female paramedic telling me to just lay down and rest, and my mom right beside me. My mom began to cry and started telling me how I had a seizure at home and she was thinking I was going to die and that she wouldn't have the chance to tell me she loved me one more time. A month later, I was officially diagnosed with epilepsy. I'll never be the same."

A Team Approach

Self-management is a term used to describe the way that people manage a chronic health problem such as epilepsy—that people actually do to manage their seizures and the way it affects their daily life. Self-management does not mean that people treat themselves! Far from it—self-management requires teamwork between health care professionals, caregivers, families, and teens. Everyone works together as "co-managers" centered around teens and families. It's important to also realize that family members may be "hidden patients" with their own needs and concerns, while they fulfill their roles as caregivers and "co-managers." This approach means that no one is going to tell parents and their teens what to do, but will put the teen and their family in the center and recommend a plan of care that will help accomplish their goals.

To make self-management work, goals of treatment are best individualized to the teens and their family. These goals may include working towards "no seizures and no side effects" in a manner that supports teen empowerment, yet also work towards improving the quality of life for teens and their families.

Managing epilepsy requires that everyone have a "working knowledge" of seizures, but more importantly, that they know what to do to implement the plan of care! Caregivers and families need accurate information, the "how to" skills and strategies, and the appropriate resources and support to make it all work. A psychosocial model of epilepsy self-management suggests that critical needs or components extend beyond seizures and medications to include management of safety, lifestyle, and information. In addition, teens with epilepsy must learn how epilepsy may affect their general health and what skills and resources they need to live independently.

Designing a Treatment Plan

As a child enters adolescence, parents and other caregivers design their treatment in relation to the teen's current needs and anticipate the potential problems that may develop in the future. The team may begin with just the primary care provider or neurologist. If seizures are not easily diagnosed or controlled, specialists in epilepsy care will be needed. A nurse, or other appropriate health care professional, should be incorporated to provide necessary education, skill-building, and support. However, since life with epilepsy is more than just the seizures, caring for the teen with epilepsy may also require the expertise of neuropsychologists, psychiatrists, social workers, educators, and rehabilitation therapists. Other caregivers in the community may be called upon, depending on the teen's needs, such as a school nurse, guidance counselor, camp counselor, employment specialist, personal care attendants, or respite care workers.

Making this work involves figuring out what kind of decision-making process that families and teens prefer. For example, do they prefer that the doctor or other professional be the "authority" and assume control? Or do the teen and parents work best when control and decision-making is a shared process? Understanding the roles and power of each person will help the team communicate more effectively.

Teens with epilepsy need family support because they face additional problems of seizures interfering with their physical, emotional, and social life. (© Trinity Mirror/ Mirrorpix/Alamy)

Successful Epilepsy Care

There is no recipe for successful epilepsy care. However, research in epilepsy and other chronic illnesses have suggested a number of very important factors to consider. A person's self-confidence (also called self-efficacy) has been shown repeatedly to influence how well a person manages and copes with chronic illness, including medication management for epilepsy. The ability to talk with the doctor, make shared decisions, and feel empowered are aspects of communication that may help a person move from asking questions to taking action. Being satisfied with their care and having support from others influences a person's self-confidence and ability to manage seizures. Likewise, a person's mood influences their confidence, as well as their feelings and reactions to stigma, a problem common for many teens with seizures. When mood problems such as these are present, a person's ability to manage their health may also be affected, thus emphasizing the need to identify and treat mood problems early. Lastly, tailoring goals and treatment empowers each person to be in charge, to be responsible, and to rake action. Unfortunately many barriers to obtaining care exist, such as lack of health care resources, insurance, or transportation, as well as social and cultural barriers among different groups of people. Making epilepsy care work for teens will depend upon finding ways to overcome these barriers, while building on successful self-management approaches.

The adolescent years are a time of many changes, conflicts, and growing independence. Teens living with seizures will face additional challenges that require good working relationships and communication between parents, health care providers and teens. The self-management approach can be used to facilitate this relationship and help families and caregivers organize their needs, implement plans, and teach teens how to manage their epilepsy.

CHAPTER 2

Issues and Controversies Concerning Epilepsy

Drugs May Be Able to Prevent Trauma-Related Epilepsy

Lauran Neergaard

Traumatic brain injuries (TBIs) resulting from car crashes or war wounds are a significant cause of epilepsy, reports Associated Press writer Lauran Neergaard in the following selection. But it can be difficult to recognize when and how epilepsy develops in patients with TBIs because the early symptoms of the disorder are often subtle. The injured brain may experience a "silent period" free of seizures before epilepsy emerges, the author points out. Some research suggests that newer antiepileptic drugs might prevent epilepsy in people with brain injuries if they start treatment with these drugs early in the healing process. Specialists urge increased public awareness about the risk of epilepsy for people with TBIs so that they may better treat—and perhaps even prevent—the onset of seizures.

Photo on previous page. The issues and controversies surrounding diagnosis and treatment of epilepsy with drugs has risen in recent years. **(Phanie/Photo Researchers, Inc.)**

Survivors of traumatic brain injuries—from car-crash victims to soldiers wounded in Iraq—face an extra hurdle as they recover: Thousands of them will develop epilepsy months or years later. The risk is

SOURCE: Lauran Neergaard, "Doctors Trying to Prevent Trauma-Related Epilepsy Risk," *Wisconsin State Journal,* April 3, 2007, p. A7. Copyright © 2007 Capital Newspapers. Reproduced by permission.

especially high for certain kinds of war injures. Studies of Vietnam veterans suggest up to 50 percent, says Dr. Nancy Temkin of the University of Washington.

Major new research is looking into ways to predict exactly who is most at risk and how to protect their vulnerable brains. Among the efforts [are] pilot studies to see if the newer seizure-treating drugs Topamax or Keppra might actually prevent epilepsy if they're taken immediately after a serious brain injury.

"It is among the most frustrating things in medicine to know that someone's at risk . . . and be unable to do anything about it," says Dr. Marc Dichter of the University of Pennsylvania, who is leading the Topamax study and pushing for better recognition of such patients.

When Does Epilepsy Begin?

Adding to their struggle, epilepsy may not begin with the classic jerking seizures, but instead with memory loss, attention problems or other more subtle symptoms that doctors can mistakenly attribute to the original brain injury, post-traumatic stress or some other factor.

Almost 3 million Americans have epilepsy, a condition in which the brain essentially suffers periodic electrical storms. When its circuits misfire fast enough, a seizure results.

Epilepsy has multiple causes. Some people are born with it. But about 5 percent of the nation's epilepsy was caused by traumatic brain injury, or TBI. What's the risk? Roughly 25 percent of survivors of moderate to severe brain injury will develop epilepsy. Even more, perhaps, for certain types of war injures.

Injuries that cause bleeding inside the brain are the riskiest. The population at risk is huge: Some 1.4 million children and adults suffer serious brain injuries every year from car or bike crashes, falls, gunshot wounds and other trauma.

After the initial injury, inflammation and treatment comes a "silent period" during which survivors work to recover. It can last months or even years before epilepsy appears.

"This silent period is not really silent," Dr. Shlomo Shinnar of the Albert Einstein College of Medicine told a meeting of epilepsy specialists at the National Institutes of Health [(NIH) in March 2007]. Instead, as the damaged brain tries to rewire itself—a crucial process called plasticity—misfiring circuitry can form. Injured neurons can make new connections in wrong places, or overly excitable connections. Even the brain's genes change the way they work after head injury.

"You need the plasticity for recovery. You don't want to stop it. You just want to structure it in a way that it aids recovery without causing seizures," Temkin explains.

FAST FACT

About 250,000 Americans each year will develop epilepsy as a result of a past traumatic brain injury.

Scientists Test Possible Epilepsy Preventers

It's not clear yet how to do that, so scientists instead are testing what's available—seizure-controlling drugs—as possible epilepsy preventers. Three old medications have failed. New pilot studies funded by the NIH and Defense Department are checking Topamax and Keppra, which work differently from older competitors.

"It's a bit of a shot in the dark," acknowledges Dr. Pavel Klein, who is running the Keppra study at Washington Hospital Center and Children's National Medical Center in the nation's capital. But there are some hints that these newer drugs might work, perhaps by inhibiting cell-harming chemicals wrought by post-injury inflammation, he says.

Each study is enrolling about 90 patients, a first step to ensure the drugs won't harm overall recovery before larger trials begin. Participants get the drug within hours of arriving at the emergency room, and take it for one to three months. Klein has treated 60 patients so far with no serious side effects; Dichter's study at Penn begins enrolling soon.

Until some protection is found, Dichter wants a bigger effort at warning about the epilepsy risk so that patients can recognize subtle symptoms. At his urging, the American Epilepsy Society is creating a task force to target brain-injured soldiers, work that Dichter says may eventually translate to the far bigger population of injured civilians.

Consider Denise Pease, an assistant comptroller for New York City. Months after what was initially deemed a minor head injury in a 1995 taxi crash, she began experiencing lost periods of time, increasing confusion and cognitive problems.

Studies of new epilepsy drugs such as Keppra are ongoing and may be successful where other, older drugs have failed. (JB Reed/Bloomberg News/Landov)

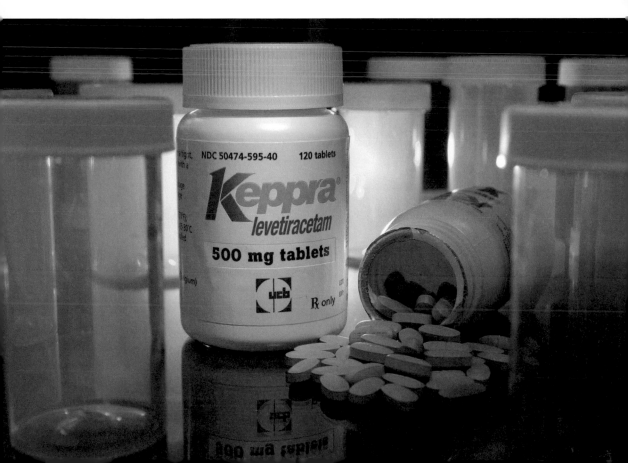

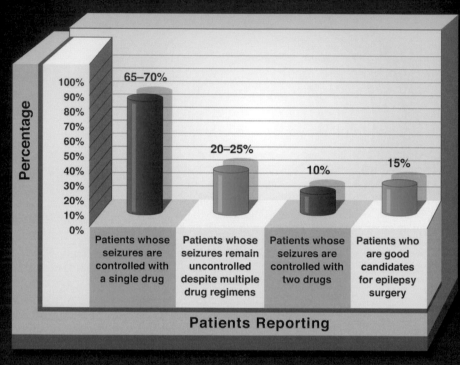

Drug Therapy and Seizure Control

Percentage

- 100%
- 90%
- 80%
- 70%
- 60%
- 50%
- 40%
- 30%
- 20%
- 10%
- 0%

65–70% — Patients whose seizures are controlled with a single drug

20–25% — Patients whose seizures remain uncontrolled despite multiple drug regimens

10% — Patients whose seizures are controlled with two drugs

15% — Patients who are good candidates for epilepsy surgery

Patients Reporting

Taken from: Renée L. Rose et al., *Drug Topics*, July 25, 2005.

Only when a nephew witnessed a muscle-jerking seizure well over a year later did she get the right diagnosis and begin her recovery. Today, after years of trying different medications, she has good epilepsy control, and warns that "my experience . . . is not unique."

Antiepileptic Drugs Can Have Negative Consequences

Jillene Magill-Lewis

Despite the advent of new and improved antiepileptic drugs (AEDs), up to 40 percent of people with epilepsy still experience seizures, writes Jillene Magill-Lewis in the following viewpoint. Moreover, researchers report serious adverse side effects associated with AEDs, including glaucoma, birth defects, cognitive impairment, osteoporosis, and an increased risk of cancer and suicide. While the treatment of epilepsy has greatly improved over the past century—and while pharmacologists continue to develop better therapies—AEDs are not complication-free, the author concludes. Magill-Lewis is a clinical writer based in Seattle, Washington.

Although epilepsy is the "oldest medical condition known to humankind, it is still surrounded in mystery, ignorance, and fear," said Eric R. Hargis,

SOURCE: Jillene Magill-Lewis, "Taking Control of Epilepsy: New Antiepileptic Drugs Are on the Horizon to Help Treat this Primordial Medical Condition Shrouded in Mystery and Fear," *Drug Topics,* vol. 150, March 6, 2006, p. 30. Copyright © 2006. *Drug Topics* is a copyrighted publication of Advanstar Communications, Inc. All rights reserved. Reprinted with permission from *Drug Topics.*

president and CEO [chief executive officer] of the Epilepsy Foundation. Despite great advances in diagnosis and treatment, there are still people with undiagnosed epilepsy, patients suffering with adverse effects, and patients without complete control of their seizures.

"At the end of the day, 30% to 40% of patients still have seizures," explained Barry Gidal, Pharm.D., professor of pharmacy and neurology, School of Pharmacy, University of Wisconsin–Madison. Even one seizure is too many, added Rex S. Lott, Pharm.D., associate professor of pharmacy practice and administrative pharmacy at Idaho State University College of Pharmacy, where he specializes in psychiatric and neurologic pharmacy.

Current medications simply are not meeting the needs of all people with epilepsy. "This usually occurs either because the meds don't work for them or because they're unable to tolerate the side effects," Lott said. . . .

FAST FACT

Currently available antiepileptic drugs are still inadequate for a significant number of patients with epilepsy.

The Cons of Drug Therapy

It's fairly safe to say that treating epilepsy is far better than leaving it untreated. Treatment improves the health and quality of life of people with the disorder. Unfortunately, treatment is not without complications. Nearly every AED [antiepileptic drug], old and new, is associated with drowsiness, dizziness, and lethargy. The older AEDs have well-documented adverse effects, while newer AEDs are touted for being tolerated much better.

The newer AEDs are not completely benign, however. Lamotrigine's prescribing information carries a black box warning about rare but potentially life-threatening rashes. Gabapentin may cause glaucoma with long-term use, and studies have associated it with a possible increased risk for cancer. Both gabapentin and levetiracetam may need dosage reductions to allow for renal function impairment, if present.

Newer Epilepsy Drugs and Their Side Effects

Drug	Symptom				
	Fatigue	Dizziness	Weakness	Anxiety	Insomnia
Felbatol					✓
Gabitril	✓	✓	✓	✓	
Keppra	✓		✓		
Lamictal		✓			✓
Necrontin	✓	✓			
Topamax	✓	✓		✓	
Trileptal	✓	✓			
Zarontin					
Zonegran		✓			

Drug	Symptom				
	Rash	Confusion	Weight Loss	Headaches	Vision Problems
Felbatol			✓	✓	
Gabitril		✓			
Keppra					
Lamictal	✓				
Necrontin					
Topamax		✓	✓	✓	✓
Trileptal				✓	✓
Zarontin			✓		
Zonegran	✓			✓	

Taken from: R. Morgan Griffin, WebMD Epilepsy Health Center, August 1, 2006.

Other serious adverse events, such as birth defects, suicide, cognitive impairment, and even seizures, have all been associated with AED use. Drug registries track and document adverse events, including birth defects. Data compiled from five AED registries suggest that valproate and phenobarbital are both associated with increased risks of birth defects and developmental disorders. Although there are fewer data on newer AEDs, early evidence is that some of the newer AEDs are less likely to cause birth defects.

According to Martha Morrell, M.D., clinical professor of neurology, Stanford University, children of women taking lamotrigine may have no greater risk of birth defects than those in the general population. "We hope more information will be available soon about other newer AEDs. Then, we'll be in a better position to understand how to use them with women of childbearing age."

Adverse Effects on Cognition and Everyday Functions

Children with epilepsy are prone to effects on cognition, both from epilepsy and the drugs used to treat it. Children with epilepsy may have changes in attention, memory, mental speed, language, and behavior. Studies are under way to measure just how much the disorder affects cognition in children and what role AEDs may play.

Children aren't the only patients plagued by cognitive adverse effects. Surveys of adults have revealed that drowsiness, lethargy, memory loss, and mood swings have had major impacts on their lives. Respondents reported these adverse effects had prevented them from participating in certain activities and achieving goals. Some reported adverse effects on job performance. When asked about specific drug regimens, patients reported more side effects with polytherapy [a combination of drugs] than monotherapy.

AEDs are used off label to treat other disorders, such as migraine headaches, bipolar disorder, neuropathic pain, and insomnia. In addition to the usual adverse ef-

People being treated for epilepsy are subject to debilitating side effects such as depression and fatigue. (© [apply pictures]/Alamy)

fects that can be expected with AEDs, the drugs may also cause seizures in people who don't normally have them. [In 2005], Cephalon added a warning to this effect to the prescribing information for tiagabine (Gabitril).

"The suicide rate for epilepsy patients is higher than you'd expect with the general population," Gidal said. The reason for this remains unknown. "We know that depression occurs commonly in people with epilepsy and that depression is associated with a risk of suicide," said

Lott. The link between AEDs and suicide is unclear. The FDA [Food and Drug Administration] has asked AED manufacturers to look at clinical data and find out what, if any, suicide risk may be associated with the AEDs they make. The FDA is following a protocol similar to that used when reexamining antidepressants for suicidal risk.

"The way things stand, there's no evidence that any of the AEDs cause suicide," said Gidal. Unless and until there is evidence to the contrary, he recommended that pharmacists recognize there is a fair amount of depression associated with epilepsy and monitor patients accordingly. Pharmacists can assess for mood changes, recognize them, and suggest they be addressed.

Epilepsy Patients Can Have Better Quality of Life

Treatment of epilepsy has vastly improved over the past century. It is far from perfect, but with continued research will come even more effective and better-tolerated treatments. Unfortunately, many patients still are not taking advantage of newer treatments. This is mostly out of habit, said Gidal, both on the part of patients and physicians. Also, the old adage "If it ain't broke, don't fix it" seems to be the mantra of many. However, some things that may be broken may not be easily recognized. For example, patients may have already accommodated for some cognitive effects. Other effects, like osteoporosis, aren't readily recognizable without testing.

Fears of seizures that can occur during a switch in medication can also discourage improvements in therapy. The best way to prevent all this, said Gidal, is to be proactive. When starting younger people on an AED, choose one that will be good for long-term use. Look down the road to a time when polypharmacy, osteoporosis, and so on may be issues. When AEDs are thoroughly and carefully evaluated and selected, people of all ages who suffer from epilepsy can look forward to better seizure control and quality of life.

Generic Drugs May Be Dangerous for People with Epilepsy

Donna Wright

Pharmacists should be required to notify patients with epilepsy before switching their prescriptions to generic drugs, argues Donna Wright in the following article. Because generic drugs are cheaper than brand-name drugs, pharmacists and health insurance plans commonly opt for the generic version of the drug over the brand name. Such a switch can have disastrous consequences for people with epilepsy, however, because some people do not readily absorb generic drugs and will end up having seizures as a result. Passing a law that requires patients with epilepsy and their doctors to be notified of any drug substitutions is crucial for both personal and public safety, Wright explains. Wright is a health and social services reporter for the *Bradenton Herald*, a Florida newspaper.

Florida lawmakers can help more than 360,000 Floridians this spring [2008] and it won't break their budget. All they have to do is pass pending bills in the House and Senate that would require pharmacists to notify and get consent from a patient and the prescribing physicians before substituting a drug for a patient with epilepsy.

For most of us, a switch to a generic drug or a substitution medication causes no problems. But for people with epilepsy, the switch can have disastrous effects, according to Dr. W. Alvin McElveen, a Bradenton neurologist and member of the American Academy of Neurology or AAN.

"I had one patient who switched to a generic to save money and ended up in the hospital with seizures," McElveen said. "Some people don't seem to absorb the generic drugs as well as the brand names."

An epileptic patient with a few of the drugs she has tried in an attempt to control her epilepsy. Insurers' plans for different drug treatments often put the patient at risk. (AP Images)

In another case, McElveen thought his patient was not taking her medications when her seizures returned. But she insisted she was. "I asked her if she was taking the little blue pill, and she said, 'No, it's a little white pill,'" McElveen said. "She had switched to a generic and that switch cost her a couple of hospitalizations."

A Potential Disaster

But McElveen recognizes drug prices can be a problem. "Some drug plans won't pay for the brand names or else they put them on a higher tier that cost more," he said. "We are even seeing some drug plans that won't put a branded drug on their formulary. Patients who don't have a lot of money want the cheaper drugs, so they go to the generics, but these can pose specific problems because the absorption rates can differ and differences in dosage can make a big difference in people's response."

> **FAST FACT**
>
> Epilepsy affects over 3 million Americans of all ages, at an estimated annual cost of $12.5 billion.

When a generic drug works, McElveen is willing to prescribe it, but he said even generics can differ in absorption rate depending on the manufacturer. "There may be four companies that make the generic drug. I may put someone on a specific generic that stabilizes their condition, but if they switch generics, there can be problems, too."

Slight variations in composition and absorption rates, which would normally have little to no effect on patients with other types of conditions, can cause life-alternating and even life-threatening breakthrough seizures for people with epilepsy, according to the Epilepsy Foundation of Florida. Dr. Basim Uthman, associate professor of Neurology and Neuroscience at the University of Florida College of Medicine, used the analogy of walking a tightrope without a safety net to describe the delicate process of finding an epilepsy patient's precise medication and dosage.

The Dangers of Switching to Generic Drugs

According to a 2008 study, half of the people with breakthrough seizures—those that occur in people whose seizures are generally well controlled—after a switch to generic antiseizure drugs were found to have dangerously low blood levels of that drug.

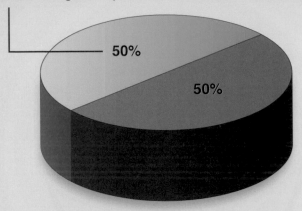

50%

50%

Taken from: Matthew Huffman, September 16, 2008. www.webmd.com.

"Small deviations to either side of the rope are highly likely to result in a major event without much warning," Uthman said in a statement supporting the bill.

For some patients, breakthrough seizures resulting from a switch in medications could lead to the loss of a job or a person's ability to work.

Noevia's Story

Consider the tragic story of Noevia Lopez of Miami.

Thanks to effective treatment with anticonvulsant drugs to control her seizures without severe side effects, Lopez not only realized her dream of becoming a dancer but rapidly rose to international fame as a Prima Balle-rina for the American Ballet Theater in New York City.

But when her medication was substituted without her knowledge or her physician's consent, she began having grand mal seizures once again. During one of these seizures Lopez fell. Her injuries were so significant she had to have a hip replacement, which ended her career.

"Just one seizure can result in a mother or father losing their driving privileges and jeopardize not only their family's lifestyle, but their livelihood," said Karen Egozi, director of the epilepsy foundation. "Worse yet, if that seizure occurs while they are driving or in a variety of other circumstances, they not only can harm themselves, but put others in harm's way as well."

Passage of proposed Senate Bill 2414 and House Bill 811 are critical to helping people with epilepsy successfully manage their condition. Quick action is also important for many of the veterans who are returning home from Iraq with massive head injuries. Head trauma is one of the leading causes of epilepsy.

Sure, budgets are tight in Tallahassee [Florida's capital], but this is one law the Legislature can afford to pass.

Surgery Can Benefit People with Epilepsy

Anita Manning

In the following selection Anita Manning tells the story of Lance Rice, a high school student and hemophiliac who developed epilepsy as an infant as a result of bleeding in his brain. At age sixteen, Lance had surgery that removed the damaged areas in his brain where the seizures originated. Doctors have reported that Lance has progressed well: He is now seizure-free and may be able to stop taking antiepileptic drugs in the future. According to Manning, friends and family note that Lance is more energetic and self-confident; he has also improved academically. He serves as an example, Manning asserts, of how such an operation can enhance the health of those with a surgically treatable form of epilepsy. Manning is a writer for the newspaper *USA Today*.

O n a warm afternoon [in the spring of 2007], Lance Rice, 17, sat in a classroom at the A-Auto Driving School along with 16 other teens going through the required classes to get their driver's licenses.

SOURCE: Anita Manning, "A Smile Returns After Rare Surgery," *USA Today*, May 9, 2007, p. 09D. Copyright © 2007, *USA Today*. Reproduced by permission.

It's an unremarkable rite of passage, except that for Lance, who has epilepsy, it's something of a miracle. Lance was born with hemophilia, and when he was just days old, he had bleeding in his brain that left him with epilepsy, a seizure disorder. Despite daily doses of three anti-epilepsy drugs, he was having at least two seizures a week. His condition affected everything from his school-work to his self-esteem.

[In the fall of 2006] Lance underwent a remarkable operation at the Cleveland Clinic. Doctors opened his skull and placed a grid of electrodes directly onto his brain. Over a period of days, they mapped the sections of the brain that control speech, movement and other func-tions and zeroed in on areas where Lance's seizures origi-nated. On Nov. 9 [2006], surgeons removed about a fifth of his brain. The operation, rarely performed on a patient with hemophilia, was covered by *USA Today*.

Lance hasn't had a seizure since.

All the Positive Things

Now, says his mother, Michelle Rice, "there is a confi-dence level I see in him that I haven't seen in a very long time."

From age 5 to 11 he had no seizures. Then, "Lance was very personable. He smiled a lot. When he had sei-zures, he just didn't seem as happy. I see a lot of that back. I see him laughing a lot more, smiling a lot more. . . . He's just happier."

There have been other changes. Lance, a bulky young man who wears baggy jeans and T-shirts, has lost 25 pounds since the operation and aims to lose 40 more. He has embarked on a fitness program that includes walking every day, bike riding and shooting baskets after school.

His parents are shopping for a car for him, and he plans to start working this summer at a local golf club. He's talking about going to college, planning to share a "party house" with his best friend and bowling buddy, Danny Cofer, 17.

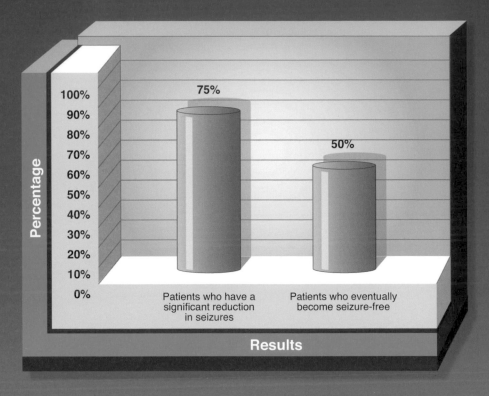

Seizure Control Among People Who Have a Second Epilepsy Surgery

Percentage

100%
90%
80%
70%
60%
50%
40%
30%
20%
10%
0%

75%

50%

Patients who have a
significant reduction
in seizures

Patients who eventually
become seizure-free

Results

Taken from: Stephen C. Schacter, ed., "Q&A Chat: Epilepsy Surgery," 2008. www.epilepsy.com.

Over a dinner at a restaurant, where Lance chooses the mahi-mahi and a glass of water, he plays it all down. His life "hasn't changed. I still get C's at school."

His mother rolls her eyes.

"What?" he says. "I still hang around with the same people."

He still speaks in a low voice and is shy with strangers. But he's different, Danny says. He's easier to talk to, no longer having to struggle through a mental fog caused partly by medication. He has energy and confidence to be more physically active, something he rarely did before, when overexertion would trigger seizures.

"He used to come home from school and every day spend at least two hours doing his homework," his mother says. "Lance used to have to really work to get C's. Now on almost every report card, there's at least two A's."

Success Means Scaling Back Medications

Lance will return to the Cleveland Clinic . . . for tests. His doctors have been checking in with the family periodically. "His progress is very satisfying," says Deepak Lachhwani, the pediatric epileptologist who oversaw the tests that identified the problem area primarily in the left frontal lobe. That area usually controls language, but in Lance's case, the damage occurred when he was so young that other parts of the brain took over that function. The goal of the surgery was to remove the damaged areas without harming sections that control movement and other functions.

Performing this type of surgery on someone with hemophilia was a first for the doctors. "From a purely epilepsy standpoint, Lance is doing as well as other kids would have done, where we found a surgically treatable form" of the disease, Lachhwani says. But "with the hemophilia, I'm pleasantly surprised that we didn't run into complications."

Lance gives himself infusions every other day of the protein factor VIII his blood needs to prevent bleeding. During his two weeks in the hospital, he received continual infusions and had no bleeding problems related to the surgery.

He takes just two anti-epilepsy drugs, and, depending on test results, he might cut back to one. "After one to two years of being seizure-free, we offer him (the option) to come totally off his seizure medicines," Lachhwani says.

There are no guarantees he will not have another seizure, but the longer he goes without one, the smaller the chance of having one.

> **FAST FACT**
>
> Many specialists maintain that a patient should be evaluated for surgery if he or she still has seizures after taking two or more anti-epileptic drugs for more than two years.

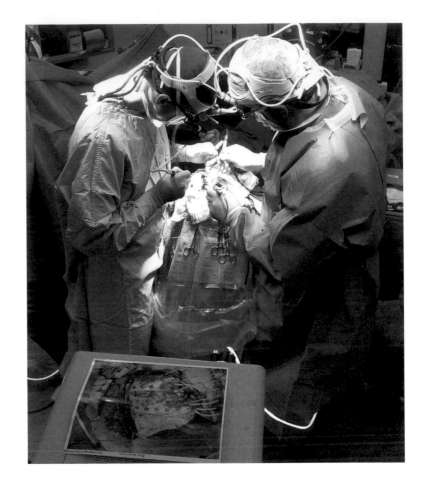

Neurosurgeons at the Children's Hospital of Pittsburgh operate on a two-year-old's brain to remove abnormal tissue that may cause seizures. (**AP Images**)

Lance's Advice

In the months since *USA Today* reported on the surgery, the support of family and friends in the hemophilia community has been overwhelming, says Michelle Rice, director of Hemophilia of Indiana. Lance's website, caringbridge.org/visit/lancerice, has had 7,500 hits. Other ailing young people share their stories.

Lance says the tests, the time in the hospital, the painful recovery and the uncertainty of the outcome all were worth going through.

Asked what advice he'd give those considering being evaluated for surgery, he doesn't hesitate: "I'd say, 'Look at me. I'm seizure-free.'"

Surgery Does Not Improve Cognitive Function in People with Epilepsy

Michele G. Sullivan

Recent research suggests that childhood epilepsy surgery does not result in improvements in cognitive function, notes Michele G. Sullivan in the following selection. A study of adults with a history of childhood epilepsy reveals that those who have surgery experience no significant changes in intellectual capacities over time. Parents who had hoped that their children's cognitive abilities would improve after surgery may find this news discouraging, the author points out. Yet these findings can also be seen in a positive light, because they also suggest that epileptic surgery poses no major risk to cognitive function. Sullivan writes articles for a variety of medical periodicals.

Childhood epilepsy surgery isn't associated with a long-term improvement in cognitive functioning, Janet Olds, Ph.D., and her colleagues reported in a poster at the joint annual meeting of the American Epilepsy Society and the American Clinical Neurophysiology Society.

SOURCE: Michele G. Sullivan, "Pediatric Epilepsy Fails to Aid Later Cognitive Function," *Clinical Psychiatry News,* vol. 34, April 2006, p. 35. Copyright © 2006 International Medical News Group. Reproduced by permission.

While findings from previous studies have shown that the surgery has no short-term effect on childhood cognition, little was known until now about its long-term effect on adult cognition, noted Dr. Olds, a psychologist at the Children's Hospital of Eastern Ontario.

The Scope of the Study

She assessed cognitive function in 50 adults (mean age 22 years) with a history of childhood epilepsy; 34 had undergone epilepsy surgery at least 2 years prior to assessment.

Of these, 21 were seizure-free and 13 continued to have seizures. The other 16 subjects, who served as controls, had never had surgery for their epilepsy as children and continued to have seizures as adults.

Seizure-free surgical subjects were taking a mean of one antiepileptic drug. Both the surgical group with continued seizures and the nonsurgical group were taking a mean of two antiepileptic drugs.

FAST FACT

Potential complications of childhood epilepsy surgery include stroke, language impairment, and paralysis.

All of the subjects completed a neuropsychological assessment consisting of measures of intelligence, memory, and executive functioning (Wechsler Adult Intelligence Scale, vocabulary and block design; Wechsler Memory Scale, logical memory and memory for faces; Wisconsin Card Sort Test). Scores were compared with the subjects' pre- and postsurgical scores on the same tests.

There were no group differences in problem solving as reflected in the Wisconsin Card Sort Test. Surgery subjects who continued to have seizures scored lower on vocabulary and verbal memory tests, compared with both the seizure-free surgery group and the no-surgery group.

When the scores in two surgical groups were compared, the seizure-free group did better on vocabulary and block design, compared with the group still having

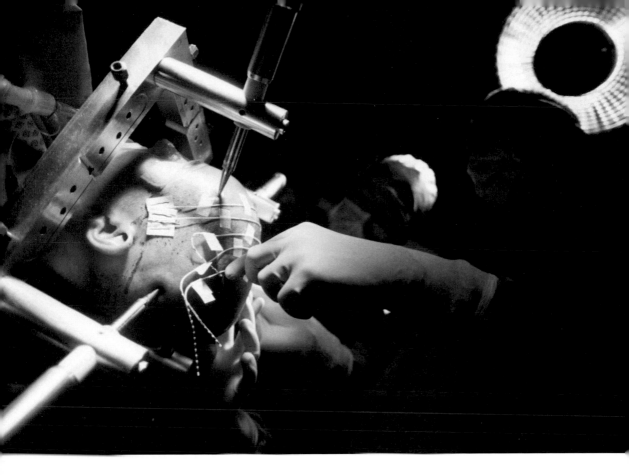

seizures. However, there were no differences in scores across the three test periods, indicating no significant change in functioning over time.

A surgeon implants electrodes into an epileptic patient's brain by way of a procedure known as stereoelectroen-cephalography (SEEG). **(Phanie/Photo Researchers Inc.)**

The News Is Good or Bad

It's important to include a discussion of cognitive function when counseling parents about the potential impact of epilepsy surgery, said Mary Lou Smith, Ph.D., the study's principal investigator. The majority of research suggests that cognitive skills won't change—a fact that can be construed in a positive, as well as potentially negative, light.

"In essence, this is good news, although not necessarily the good news those parents would like to hear," Dr. Smith, of the University of Toronto, said in an interview. "[Parents] may wish, and often do, that their child will show improved cognitive function after surgery."

The Age of Patients at Epilepsy Onset

70%
of people with epilepsy
develop the disorder
before age 20

30%
develop epilepsy after
20 years of age

Taken from: GP, "Diagnosis and Management of Epilepsy Basics," December 14, 2007.

She added that it is important to remember that the study's conclusions are based on group numbers and that within each group, some children do better or worse than the study's findings indicate.

Unfortunately, Dr. Smith said, there's no consensus on what factors predict who will improve and who will deteriorate. "The few studies that have included a comparison group of children with intractable epilepsy who don't have surgery show that the proportion who shows increases or decreases is the same in both surgical and nonsurgical groups," she commented.

The general conclusion is that as long as the eloquent cortex remains intact, there is no particular cognitive risk or benefit associated with the surgery, said Dr. Smith.

Brain Stimulation Can Benefit People with Epilepsy

Ken Carlson

Electric brain stimulation may help to control epilepsy in patients who have had mixed results with conventional therapies, reports Ken Carlson in the following viewpoint. Carlson outlines the case of Shannen Soldate, who continued to have seizures while taking medication and after the surgical removal of a scarred area of her brain thought to be the source of her epilepsy. In 2006 Soldate joined a clinical trial of the NeuroPace Responsive Neurostimulator System (RNS), a device that is implanted under the scalp. The RNS can contain or stop a seizure by sending low-intensity electrical current to trouble spots in the brain. Soldate is not entirely seizure-free, Carlson notes, but she has not had a major seizure since the RNS device was implanted. Carlson is a reporter for the *Modesto Bee*, a California daily newspaper.

For more than 22 years, Shannen Soldate of Oakdale [California] tried medications to control seizures that left her exhausted, caused her to miss work and made her afraid to go out. Now a small computer

SOURCE: Ken Carlson, "Better Control of Epilepsy Is Under the Scalp," *The Modesto Bee*, August 25, 2008. Copyright © 2008 *The Modesto Bee*. Reproduced by permission.

under her scalp, with sensors leading into her brain, is treating her epilepsy with better results. Soldate, 39, is one of hundreds of patients testing a first generation of brain stimulation systems that could relieve suffering for many with epilepsy. Her shoulder-length hair conceals the computer, and she can't feel the electrical pulses delivered in her brain. "There were times I was having 15 seizures a day," she said. "I don't have grand mal seizures anymore. I'm not as worried that I'm going to have a seizure in public. I'm a little more optimistic."

The device, called the NeuroPace Responsive Neurostimulator System [RNS], developed by a Mountain View [California] company, is undergoing trials at 29 hospitals in the United States to test its safety and effectiveness. Soldate is a patient at the California Pacific Medical Center Epilepsy Center in San Francisco, where a trial is under way. It is not a cure for epilepsy, a disorder that afflicts 3 million people in the United States with seizures marked by confusion, disorientation, convulsions or loss of consciousness. The system is designed to detect irregular brain activity that signals the onset of a seizure and delivers an electrical stimulus to stop it cold. If it works as intended, patients don't feel the treatment.

Medicine Is Not Always Effective

Medicine controls seizures for about two-thirds of people with epilepsy, but Soldate doesn't respond well to anticonvulsant drugs. She had her first seizure when she was a 16-year-old high schooler in Petaluma [California]. She was driving a friend's car when it happened. Her friend grabbed the steering wheel and safely stopped the car. Soldate didn't tell her parents. Her family remained in the dark until her sister watched her have a seizure while taking a nap at home.

For the next 15 years, doctors gave Soldate different combinations of anti-seizure drugs. But the seizures persisted and the drugs made her drowsy, slurred her speech and caused her hands to shake. Despite the dis-

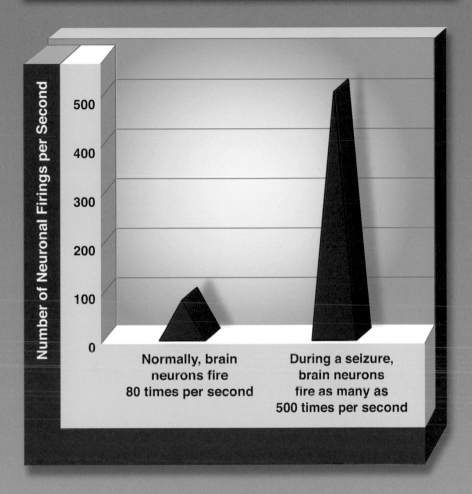

Epilepsy and Neuron Activity in the Brain

Number of Neuronal Firings per Second

500
400
300
200
100
0

Normally, brain
neurons fire
80 times per second

During a seizure,
brain neurons
fire as many as
500 times per second

Taken from: National Women's Health Resource Center, December 15, 2005.

order, she married her boyfriend, Eric, and they chose to have a child, even though the medications can cause birth defects. Although not all of her bosses were sensitive, Soldate was determined to work and spent 14 years servicing accounts in the mortgage industry. The family moved to Oakdale in 2000. During the worst of times, epilepsy caused her to miss work. And she lost her license. "You don't realize how independent you are until you lose your driver's license," she said. "To lose that was really hard."

Surgery and a Clinical Trial

In 2000, she underwent surgery at a [San Francisco] Bay Area hospital to remove scarring on a portion of her brain where the seizures originate. The surgery let her reduce her

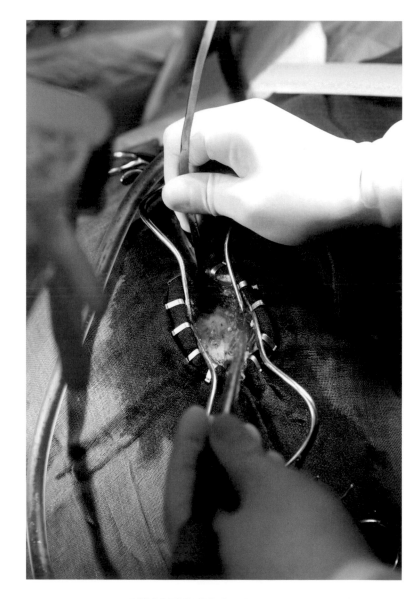

The NeuroPace Responsive Neurostimulator System is surgically implanted in the brain of a person with epilepsy. It can stop a seizure by sending electrical current to affected areas of the brain. (Phanie/Photo Researchers Inc.)

daily medications. She returned to work but had a grand mal seizure in the office. Her neurologist at the University of California San Francisco Medical Center got her interested in brain stimulation. She was the third patient enrolled in the clinical trial in September 2006.

The NeuroPace RNS is one of two brain stimulation systems undergoing trials. Both evolved from cardiac pacemakers, which deliver electrical currents to regulate heart rhythms. NeuroPace's early warning system sets it apart. It signals the device to emit low intensity electric current to stop the seizure from spreading. Surgeons implanted the electrodes in Soldate's right temporal lobe, the part of the brain where her seizures originate. She is not the only the patient to have positive results. "When the stimulus is given at the right time and intensity, it can block the seizure," said Dr. David King-Stephens, clinical director of the neurophysiology lab at California Pacific Medical Center. "The preliminary results are pretty impressive. Some patients are not having seizures, and the majority have had a 60 to 70 percent reduction in seizures. Some patients have stopped having disabling seizures."

The computer keeps a continuous record of Soldate's brain activity. Every night, she waves a wand over the implanted unit to download the information into a laptop computer that sends the data over phone lines to the epilepsy center. The information lets doctors adjust the system to achieve better results. "It's like a thumbprint," said Dr. Martha Morrell, chief medical officer for NeuroPace and a clinical professor of neurology at Stanford University. "The system is programmed to pick up the patient's seizure signature and deliver the right amount of stimulus."

No More Major Seizures

The therapy has allowed Soldate to reduce her medications from four per day to three. She is not free of seizures, though. The device has recorded up to 580 eruptions in a day, most of which she hasn't felt. She has had days when seizures came one after another. Most are what she called "absent seizures"—she gets an absent look on her face and can hear things going on around her but can't comprehend anything. She records the severity and duration of her seizures in a diary. Her last was July 23 [2008]. She hasn't experienced a major seizure since she was taken off medications in the hospital the day the device was implanted, she said. She later resumed taking some of the medications.

Experts have been concerned that long-term exposure to electrical stimulation can damage brain tissue. Candidates for the clinical trials are informed of risks, including more frequent or worsening seizures. King-Stephens said 65 patients in a safety study haven't suffered those effects after 2 1/2 to 4 1/2 years. About 200 patients are in the trial, and doctors hope to enroll 40 more in the next three or four months. It will take 18 months to analyze data and submit results to the Food and Drug Administration [FDA].

> **FAST FACT**
>
> A Mayo Clinic–sponsored study found that 78 percent of subjects receiving brain stimulation to control epilepsy experienced at least a 50 percent reduction in seizures.

Technology Will Evolve

If the FDA approves, the system will be available to all patients in two or three years. In addition to the high-tech treatments, there are new drugs on the horizon for treating epilepsy. "People can look at these as first-generation devices and expect the technology will evolve over time," said Dr. Brian Litt, an associate professor of neurology and bioengineering at the University of Pennsylvania and a member of the professional advisory board for the Epilepsy Foundation. "If it gives people a therapy that prevents them from having seizures, and they don't have side effects, that would be a home run."

Soldate is more confident now when going out in public. She and Eric enjoy watching their daughter, Jenna, play for the California Magic traveling softball team. Eric drives them to games throughout California and in other states. "Now that I'm not having as many seizures, I'm not as tired and I'm not as irritable," she said. "My family would probably say not as bitchy." Soldate is proud of her daughter's maturity in living with a parent with epilepsy. Jenna was in sixth grade the first time she watched her mother have a major seizure at home. The youngster didn't know what to do, but she soon learned the drill: Make sure her mother is on her side, that nothing is in her mouth and let her ride it out. "I just tell my friends my mom has seizures and most of them understand," said Jenna, 17.

[In September 2008], Soldate will have outpatient surgery to replace the system's battery. The power supply lasts two or three years and is being developed to last longer, Morrell said. The system is designed to treat people whose seizures begin in a specific location in the brain, Morrell said. It's less likely to help people whose seizures arise from all over the brain. Soldate plans to continue the treatment.

"I've had a lot of help from family and friends to help me get through this," she said.

Dietary Changes Can Benefit People with Epilepsy

Christen Brownlee

Traditionally, doctors have used the ketogenic diet as an alternative way to treat epileptic children's seizures. Though the ketogenic diet reduces or even eliminates seizures, doctors typically recommend it for children because of its strict eating requirements. According to the article, Johns Hopkins University began researching and testing the effects of a modified version of the Atkins diet on epileptic adults in 2002. By the first clinical visit, half the patients experienced a reduction in the frequency of their seizures by 50 percent.

A modified version of a popular high-protein, low-carbohydrate diet can significantly cut the number of seizures in adults with epilepsy, a study led by Johns Hopkins researchers suggests. The Atkins-like diet, which has shown promise for seizure control in children, may offer a new lifeline for patients when drugs and other treatments fail or cause complications.

SOURCE: Christen Brownlee, "Modified Atkins Diet Can Cut Epileptic Seizures," Newsmax.com, January 28, 2008. All Rights Reserved © 2008 NewsMax.com. Reproduced by permission.

The Ketogenic Diet

For almost a century, doctors have prescribed an eating plan called the ketogenic diet to treat children with epilepsy. This diet often consists of a short period of fasting, strictly limits fluids and drastically restricts carbohydrates. It appears to limit or even eliminate seizures, possibly by generating the buildup of ketones, compounds the body produces when it derives calories mostly from fat. Some of the largest studies to scientifically test this diet's efficacy took place at Johns Hopkins in the mid-1990s, led by pediatric neurologists John Freeman and Eileen Vining.

Why exactly the ketogenic diet works remains unknown, and it is notoriously difficult to follow, relying

The new dietary therapy, the low glycemic index treatment (LGIT), includes broccoli because of its low impact on blood glucose levels. (© mediablitzimages (uk) Limited/Alamy)

almost solely on fat and protein for calories. Consequently, doctors typically recommend it only for children, whose parents can strictly monitor their eating habits. The ketogenic diet is almost never prescribed to adults, who generally make their own food choices and often have difficulty complying with the diet's strict guidelines.

Testing a Modified Atkins Diet

In 2002, Johns Hopkins researchers began testing a modified version of the Atkins diet in children with epilepsy. The modified diet shares the high-fat focus of the ketogenic diet, prompting the body to generate ketones. However, it allows more carbohydrates and protein, doesn't limit fluids and calories, and has no fasting period. When studies showed that the new diet prevented or curtailed seizures in children, the researchers began testing it for efficacy and ease of use in adults.

Reporting on the results in the February issue of *Epilepsia,* Eric H. Kossoff, an assistant professor of neurology and pediatrics at the School of Medicine, said 30 adults with epilepsy, ages 18 to 53 years, who had tried at least two anticonvulsant drugs without success and had an average of 10 seizures per week, were placed on the modified Atkins diet. All patients were seen for free in the Johns Hopkins General Clinical Research Center.

The regimen restricted them to 15 grams of carbohydrates a day.

"That's a few strawberries, some vegetables or a bit of bread," Kossoff said. The diet offers most of its calories from fat—eggs, meats, oils and heavy cream—with as much protein and no-carb beverages as patients want.

Each day, patients kept diaries of what they ate and how many seizures they had. The researchers evaluated how each patient was doing at one, three and six months after starting the diet.

> ## FAST FACT
>
> A Johns Hopkins study has found that a high-protein, low-carbohydrate diet can significantly reduce the frequency of seizures in adults with epilepsy.

Seizure Control Among People with Epilepsy in the United States

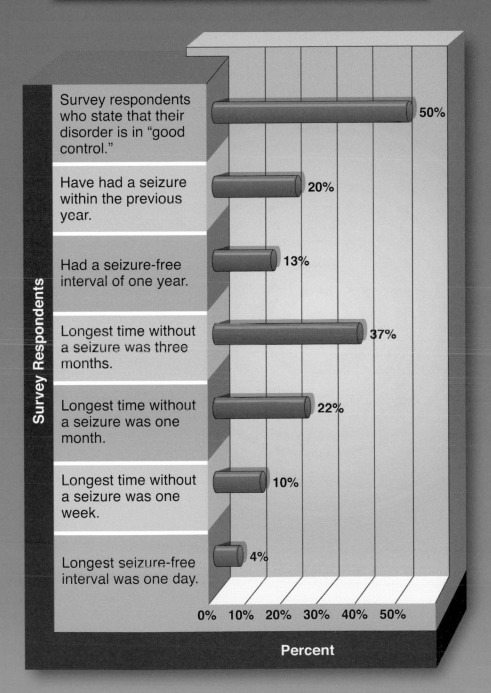

Survey Respondents

- Survey respondents who state that their disorder is in "good control." — 50%
- Have had a seizure within the previous year. — 20%
- Had a seizure-free interval of one year. — 13%
- Longest time without a seizure was three months. — 37%
- Longest time without a seizure was one month. — 22%
- Longest time without a seizure was one week. — 10%
- Longest seizure-free interval was one day. — 4%

Percent: 0% 10% 20% 30% 40% 50%

Taken from: Epilepsy Foundation, *A Report to the Nation*, 1999.

Dietary Changes Reduced Seizure Frequency

Results showed that about half the patients had experienced a 50 percent reduction in the frequency of their seizures by the first clinic visit. About a third of the patients halved the frequency of seizures by three months. Side effects linked with the diet, such as a rise in cholesterol or triglycerides, were mild. A third of the patients dropped out by the third month, unable to comply with the restrictions.

Fourteen patients who stuck with the diet until the six-month mark chose to continue, even after the study ended—a testament to how effectively the diet worked to treat their epilepsy, Kossoff notes.

Though the modified Atkins diet won't be a good fit for all patients, Kossoff said, "it opens up another therapeutic option for adults trying to decide between medication, surgery and electrical stimulation to treat intractable seizures." A second study to examine the diet's effects on adults with intractable seizures is under way.

Seizure Response Dogs Benefit People with Epilepsy

Jan Carter Hollingsworth

Seizure response dogs can help people with epilepsy live happier, more secure lives, writes Jan Carter Hollingsworth in the following selection. Carefully selected service dogs can be trained to stay close to a person who is having a seizure, summon help from others, or retrieve a phone when a person senses that she is about to have a seizure. Some dogs can even alert their owners that they will have a seizure several minutes before it happens, the author notes. By offering both physical protection and emotional support, seizure response dogs can provide people with epilepsy a sense of well-being and independence. Hollingsworth is managing editor of the *Exceptional Parent*, a magazine for parents of children with special health care needs.

In a myriad of ways, Rachel Walz is like any rambunctious six-year-old. Always on the move and with pigtails flying, she relishes athletic activity, especially riding her bike. Since October [2006] though, a golden-haired dog with the most beautiful, soft brown

SOURCE: Jan Carter Hollingsworth, "Another Tool in the Fight Against Epilepsy," *Exceptional Parent Magazine*, vol. 37, May 2007, p. 28. Copyright © 2007 EP Global Communications, Inc. Reproduced by permission.

A Study of People with Epilepsy and Their Untrained Pet Dogs

Out of sixty-three subjects with epilepsy,

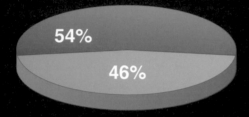

54%

46%

46% owned pet dogs.

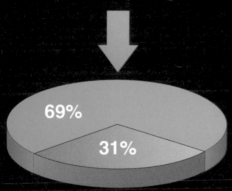

69%

31%

31% of those pet dogs reportedly responded to seizures.

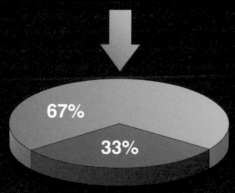

67%

33%

33% of the dogs who responded to seizures could alert the owner of an impending seizure.

Taken from: Deborah Dalziel, et al., University of Florida Veterinary Medicine Study, 1998.

eyes you've ever seen races beside her bike as Rachel tears down the driveway. Rachel, a child who is challenged with complex partial seizures as well as nausea epilepsy, has a very special companion who gives her the peace of mind and the freedom to be a regular, bicycling-riding kid. It gives her family peace of mind, too.

Epilepsy, a chronic neurological seizure disorder, affects 2.7 million Americans, half of them children, and worldwide, it is the most common brain disorder. While there is not a cure for epilepsy, the goal of treatment is to achieve the greatest freedom from seizures that can be attained with the minimal amount of side effects. These days everything from medication to diet management to surgery is used in the fight against seizures. And the Walz family, of Pitman, NJ, has added a new weapon to its seizure management arsenal in the four-legged form of a golden retriever, named Cappy, which they acquired through a non-profit organization called Canine Assistants.

Rachel's Story

At just six weeks old, baby Rachel suffered a pediatric stroke, which was followed by a seizure that complicated the stroke. Her Mom, Michele, relates, "Rachel then developed a bleed, and we were told she would probably never walk or talk." At that point, Rachel was placed on seizure medication, went eight months without a seizure and was then taken off the medication. She did, indeed, learn to walk and talk, but at age two had a full blown tonic-clonic seizure that lasted 40 minutes. This signaled the beginning of recurring seizures and ongoing experiments over the next three years with various medication combinations. "We are thrilled that, for about a year now, we have had seizure control, achieved by just the right dosage of Keppra, an anti-epileptic medication," Michele said. But like all families touched by epilepsy, seizure control is a relative term that can change in the blink of an eye. And this is where Cappy joins the story.

When asked to be Epilepsy Advocates by the medical marketing firm that works for UCB, Inc., the makers of Keppra, Rachel and her Mom were also introduced to a facility with which UCB partners, Canine Assistants. Canine Assistants was founded in 1991 and trains and provides service dogs for select children and adults with physical disabilities and other special needs. Since their partnership with UCB began in 2005, they have been especially busy training seizure response dogs.

Canine Assistants

Located 35 miles north of Atlanta, GA in the suburb of Alpharetta, Canine Assistants operates out of a multi-building complex with training rooms and kennel areas. Dogs abound here; even walking into the main office and reception area, a visitor is greeted by four furry ambassadors, "the office dogs" as they are affectionately called, who wag a cheerful greeting and say hello in that "special" way that all dogs do.

Each year over 50 golden retrievers and Labrador retrievers (and even the occasional full size poodle) learn the ropes of seizure assistance. According to Canine Assistants founder, Jennifer Arnold, most of the dogs are bred at the facility. The male and the female breeder dogs are handpicked based on their personality traits, temperament and general health. "Females have a total of four litters of pups, spaced out about every 16 months, and are then adopted and live out the rest of their lives as family pets," Jennifer says. Training literally begins as soon as puppies are born. "By the time the puppies are two days old, we actually have a team of volunteers in place to begin handling them. Just by holding a puppy in certain positions and observing their interaction with people, the trainers can begin to determine if the puppy has the personality to be a good service dog," Jennifer explains.

> **FAST FACT**
>
> About 120 service dog training organizations are in the United States. Fewer than 20 work with seizure assistance dogs.

By the time the puppies are six weeks old, they have already been introduced to over 20 commands. They are taught an amazing 91 commands during their full 64 week training program; everything from the command "Light," which tells the dog to flip the light switch with its nose, to "Careful," which cautions the dog to prepare for a precarious situation. Canine Assistants has an outstanding graduation rate with over 95 percent of their dogs successfully graduating from the program. Jennifer attributes this to the highly structured nature of the training program and the fact that training begins when the puppies are newborns. She also feels that their policy of keeping littermates together after they are taken from their mother at five weeks is an important factor in their development and well being.

The Bond Between Dog and Person

A dog is awarded to its "person" before the dog is two years old. While Jennifer admits that there is some disagreement among those in the assistance animal field on this issue, she feels that placing a dog sometime between its first and second birthday is beneficial as "you get a really unique bond between the dog and their new person when there is still something of the puppy left in them."

Anyone interested in being placed with a Canine Assistants seizure response dog must fill out an application. Applicants are evaluated on an individual basis and then contacted by Canine Assistants if they are accepted. Dogs and recipients meet for the first time at a two-week camp (six camps are held each year) that all recipients must attend. Once accepted into the program, all costs for training and lifetime care of the dogs, including veterinary care, recurrent training, and even food, if needed, are funded through private and corporate donations with no costs passed on to the recipients. Canine Assistants can even provide financial aid to cover the expenses associated with attending the two-week camp, such as travel, meals, and lodging, if the need exists. Much of the support that makes this possible comes from UCB and shows the company's commitment to developing and backing programs that enrich the lives of those who are challenged with epilepsy.

In October 2006, Rachel Walz and her mom arrived at Canine Assistants still basking in the glow of having been accepted into the program. From the second Rachel and Cappy touched hand to paw, they were friends. Michele says, "Cappy's presence in our family has brought a greater sense of normalcy to life. For instance, before Cappy's arrival, when Rachel would be downstairs and I was upstairs, I would constantly be going to the top of the stairs and calling down to her. 'Rachel, are you ok, honey?' Now I know Cappy is watching out for her and will alert me immediately if Rachel starts seizing." And herein lies the added training that seizure response dogs get over and above that received by other types of service dogs. Following general training, seizure response dogs are trained to perform one of the following behaviors, depending on the recipient's need: remain next to the person during the course of a seizure, summon help in a controlled environment, or retrieve a phone prior to the seizure when indicated by the recipient. Some documented cases even exist of seizure response dogs developing the ability to predict and react in advance to an oncoming seizure. One University of Kentucky study reported that trained dogs are able to provide overt signals alerting their owners of pending seizures up to 45 minutes prior to the event.

Physical Protection and Emotional Support

Rachel is a patient of Dr. Michael H. Goodman, a Clinical Assistant Professor of Pediatrics and Neurology at Jefferson Medical College in Philadelphia, PA and a member of the professional advisory board of the Epilepsy Foundation for Eastern Pennsylvania. Dr. Goodman believes in using ev-

Programs like Canine Assistants train companion dogs that offer people with epilepsy emotional support and physical protection. (**Lawrence Migdale/Photo Researchers Inc.**)

ery means available in aiding his patients with epilepsy and noted that seizure response dogs offer individuals with seizures "physical protection but also emotional support and protection as the family or an individual feels like they are doing something, they are being proactive in dealing with seizures and in lessening the possibility of injury during a seizure." He went on to mention, "My goal as a physician caring for patients with seizures is to control the seizures in the best way possible and . . . by making patients aware of all the tools that exist, like seizure response dogs, that will offer them the greatest sense of well being and greatest level of independence that is possible." He recognizes that "sometimes the practice of medicine has the potential for side effects for patients, from medications and other things, but having a dog by a person's side, looking out for them— there is very little down side to that."

With the support of her family, her physicians, and, of course, Cappy, Rachel isn't slowing down for anyone or anything, especially not for epilepsy. Her mother, Michele, experienced the same fears that so many parents feel when a child is first diagnosed with epilepsy. "When Rachel was diagnosed, I was afraid that a 'normal' life would not be available to her, but my view has changed completely since then. There is no grass growing under Rachel's feet, and epilepsy hasn't stopped her from doing anything."

Jennifer Arnold's Story

Jennifer Arnold, Executive Director of Canine Assistants, is no stranger to adversity. Following a diagnosis of multiple sclerosis at the age of 16, which led to wheelchair confinement, Jennifer sought the help of a canine assistant. After being denied a companion from an organization in California, she and her father, an Atlanta physician, decided to start their own canine program in Georgia. Tragically, her father was killed by a drunk driver just three weeks later.

The loss of her father left Jennifer and her mother without the means to immediately begin the canine assistants program. Nearly ten years later in 1991, Jennifer and her mother finally realized their dream of opening Canine Assistants. Jennifer readily admits that Canine Assistants is, for her, a complete "work of heart" and that the Canine Assistants program is her way of fighting "the very mean world" that the painful experiences of her youth introduced her to.

Arnold currently operates Canine Assistants with the help of her brother, Gary, her husband, Kent, who serves as the resident veterinarian, and hundreds of volunteers.

Fear of Discrimination Keeps Many People with Epilepsy Out of the Workplace

University of Florida News

According to the following article from the *University of Florida News*, a significant percentage of people with epilepsy do not apply for jobs because they believe they will face discrimination in the workplace. Even though it is illegal for employers to discriminate on the basis of disability, some employers do hesitate to hire or promote a person with epilepsy. But epilepsy is well controlled in the majority of cases, the article points out, and people with epilepsy are just as productive—in some cases even more productive—than other employees. The author concludes that health professionals should encourage patients with epilepsy to seek out fulfilling work despite fears they may have about perceived or real discrimination.

T he unemployment rate among people with epilepsy is considerably higher than the national average—not necessarily because they have frequent seizures or can't find jobs but because many continue to

SOURCE: Pat McGhee, "UF Study Reveals Fear of Discrimination Keeps Many People with Epilepsy Out of the Workplace," *University of Florida News,* December 12, 2006. Copyright © 2006 University of Florida. Reproduced by permission.

fear workplace discrimination, a new University of Florida [UF] study reveals.

The fear of discrimination at work was the major reason cited for continuing unemployment when UF researchers interviewed nearly 300 patients with epilepsy in northeast Florida and southeast Georgia in September 2005. Only about a third of patients in the study were employed. . . .

The author cites a report that says that people with epilepsy in the workplace do not have substantially more accidents than people without epilepsy. (AP Images)

A Complex Problem

The study, described in the journal *Epilepsy & Behavior*, describes a complex problem, said principal author Dr. Ramon Bautista, an assistant professor of neurology and director of the Comprehensive Epilepsy Program at the UF College of Medicine–Jacksonville. "The problem encompasses employers and companies who hire these people as well as the patients themselves, who may or may not want to work in the first place," Bautista said. "Even though the Americans with Disabilities Act makes it illegal to discriminate on the basis of one's disability, there are still employers who may think twice about hiring someone with epilepsy."

> **FAST FACT**
>
> For an employer to inquire about a job applicant's medical conditions before making a job offer is illegal.

More than 2.7 million Americans live with epilepsy, a disorder in which nerve cells in the brain misfire, sometimes causing them to lose control of body movements.

In the study, UF researchers asked patients about age, gender and race, and also about seizure frequency and the types of medications they took. In addition, they surveyed study participants about their employment status.

The survey addressed a whole range of issues—whether patients worked, if they worked full time or part time, if they had previous work experience, how important working was for them both personally and financially, how supportive their family was of their working and how much they feared workplace discrimination.

The Effects of Discrimination

"As medical practitioners, we understand why persons who have bad seizures, who are maintained on several seizure medications or have had epilepsy for many years, are less inclined to work—that didn't surprise us," he said. "(But) our study shows that if they perceive they are discriminated against at work, they're not going to work—whether rightly or wrongly. Likewise, if patients have a low personal regard for work, they will likely remain unemployed, even if their medical condition is stable."

The study revealed that 40 percent of the participants feared workplace discrimination, while only 60 percent of those surveyed—including those whose seizures were controlled—regarded work as an opportunity for personal growth and fulfillment. These fears were the main factors associated with unemployment.

The study did not document the types of discrimination experienced or feared, but discrimination typically takes many forms, Bautista said. "Discrimination can occur in hiring practices and advancement in the workplace," he said.

"It very well may be only perceived rather than actual discrimination, but if epilepsy patients believe that they have less of a chance in the workplace, then they're less likely to even want to try to work," he added.

The study findings are important because they strongly suggest that people with epilepsy face major challenges in gaining and retaining employment, said Dr. Elson So, a neurology professor and director of the Section of Electroencephalography at Mayo Clinic College of Medicine.

Epilepsy Patients' Needs Are Not Confined to Medicine

So, who has published research on employment after epilepsy surgery, cited several important things the public and physicians should know about epilepsy and employment.

"First, epilepsy in most persons is well-controlled and, as a group, occupation-related accident rates in persons with epilepsy are not substantially greater than persons without epilepsy," he said. "In addition, the productivity of persons with epilepsy is as good—and often better—than other persons, and, finally, for persons whose seizures are not fully controlled, employment conditions must be evaluated on a case-by-case basis, because workplace accommodations can usually be made if necessary," he said.

The Two Most Common Types of Seizures

Partial (Focal) Seizures
◆ May cause numbness or jerking of limbs.
◆ Often include sensations such as flashing lights, particular tastes, and noises.
◆ May include brief loss of consciousness.

Generalized Seizures	
Grand Mal Seizures	**Petit Mal (Absence) Seizures**
◆ Loss of consciousness.	◆ A short period of staring, fluttering eyelids, or facial twitching
◆ Rigidity of muscles followed by a few minutes of violent rhythmic jerking.	◆ Lasts 10–30 seconds.
◆ A few minutes of deep sleep before returning to consciousness.	◆ Usually there is no memory of the seizure.

Taken from: Phyllis G. Cooper, "Seizures," *Clinical Reference System*, 2008.

UF researchers say that as the treatment and control of epilepsy continues to improve, health-care professionals need to look beyond the clinical disorder itself and encourage and help their patients return to the workforce.

"For many people, work is an important part of life—there's a sense of fulfillment that comes with being employed," Bautista said. "It would be a shame if we in the health-care profession ignored that and focused on just the medical needs of our patients."

Laws Protect People with Epilepsy from Workplace Discrimination

U.S. Equal Employment Opportunity Commission

The following selection, excerpted from a document by the U.S. Equal Employment Opportunity Commission (EEOC), outlines some of the legal rights that protect people with epilepsy from workplace discrimination. It clarifies if and when job applicants should inform a potential employer of their epilepsy, to what extent medical information should be kept confidential, and the kinds of workplace accommodations an employee with epilepsy may need. In addition, this document explains how an employer should handle safety concerns about epilepsy and ways to ensure that no employee is harassed because of epilepsy. The EEOC is the U.S. governmental agency that enforces federal antidiscrimination laws.

The Americans with Disabilities Act (ADA) is a federal law that prohibits discrimination against individuals with disabilities. Title I of the ADA covers employment by private employers with 15 or more employees as well as state and local government employ-

SOURCE: "Questions and Answers About Epilepsy in the Workplace and the Americans with Disabilities Act," The U.S. Equal Employment Opportunity Commission, 2008. Reproduced by permission.

ers of the same size. Section 501 of the Rehabilitation Act provides the same protections for federal employees and applicants for federal employment. In addition, most states have their own laws prohibiting employment discrimination on the basis of disability. Some of these state laws may apply to smaller employers and provide protections in addition to those available under the ADA.

The U.S. Equal Employment Opportunity Commission (EEOC) enforces the employment provisions of the ADA. This document explains how the ADA might apply to job applicants and employees with epilepsy. . . .

General Information About Epilepsy

About 2.3 million people in the United States or one percent of the population have some form of epilepsy, with more than 180,000 new cases diagnosed each year in Americans of all races and ages. Epilepsy is a general term that includes various types of seizures. A seizure happens when abnormal electrical activity in the brain causes an involuntary change in body movement or function, sensation, awareness, or behavior. People diagnosed with epilepsy have had more than one seizure, and they may have had more than one kind of seizure. A seizure can last from a few seconds to a few minutes. Some individuals recover immediately from a seizure, while others may be dazed and sleepy for a period of time following a seizure. The severity of epilepsy and the type of seizure vary from person to person. For most people with epilepsy, no single cause has been determined. Seizures may result from illness (including high fever), head trauma, stroke, brain tumor, poisoning, infection, inherited conditions, brain disorders, or problems during fetal development.

Individuals with epilepsy successfully perform all types of jobs, including heading corporations, teaching and caring for children, and working in retail and customer service positions. Individuals with epilepsy also can perform jobs that might be considered "high-risk," such as police officer, firefighter, welder, butcher, and construction worker. Yet, many employers wrongly assume that people with epilepsy automatically should be excluded from certain jobs. For example, many employers believe that anyone with epilepsy cannot safely operate certain types of machinery, drive, or use computers. The reality is that because antiseizure medications and other treatment methods totally control seizures for more than half of the people with epilepsy, many employers do not know when someone in the workplace has this condition. Some people whose epilepsy is not completely controlled experience a sensation or warning called an "aura" that lets them know that they are about to have a seizure. Many other people with epilepsy only have seizures while asleep (nocturnal seizures) or seizures that do not cause loss of consciousness or motor control.

Some employers also fear hiring individuals with epilepsy because they are concerned about higher workplace insurance rates or believe that employees with epilepsy will use a lot of sick leave. Workplace insurance rates, however, are determined by how hazardous the type of work is and by an employer's overall claims record in the past, not by the physical condition of individual employees. There is no evidence that people with epilepsy are more prone to accidents on the job than anyone else. Finally, because medications usually can control seizures for most people, they do not need to take time off from work because of their epilepsy.

When Is Epilepsy a Disability?

Epilepsy is a disability when it substantially limits one or more of a person's major life activities. Major life activities are basic activities that an average person can perform with little or no difficulty, such as walking, seeing, hearing, speaking, breathing, performing manual tasks, caring for oneself, learning, and working. Major life activities also include thinking, concentrating, interacting with others, reproduction, and sleeping.

Epilepsy may be a disability because of limitations that occur as the result of seizures or because of side effects or complications that can result from medications used to "control" the condition.

Example: A court concluded that an individual who had brain surgery to control seizures, but still continued to experience two or three seizures per month, was an individual with a disability because she was substantially limited in several major life activities, such as walking, seeing, hearing, speaking, and working, while having a seizure and often was limited in caring for herself (sometimes for more than a day) following particularly severe seizures.

Example: Some individuals take drugs that control their seizures but make them drowsy, unable to concentrate, or unable to sleep. An individual who is substantially limited in major life activities such as sleeping, thinking, concentrating, or caring for himself as a result of these side effects would have a disability under the ADA.

Epilepsy also may be a disability because it was substantially limiting some time in the past (i.e., before seizures were controlled).

Example: A job applicant has had epilepsy for five years. For the past three years she has been seizure-free, but prior to that she experienced severe and unpredictable seizures. As a result, she had to move back home with her parents because she could not live alone, she was unable to drive, and rarely socialized with friends because she feared having a seizure in public. Even if the individual's epilepsy is not now substantially limiting, it substantially limited major life activities such as caring for herself and interacting with others in the past. This individual has a record of a disability.

Finally, epilepsy is a disability when it does not significantly affect a person's everyday activities, but the employer treats the individual as if it does.

Example: An employer who refuses to hire someone with epilepsy because it assumes the individual is incapable of working without hurting himself or others regards the individual as having a disability.

Under the ADA, the determination of whether an individual has a disability is made on a case-by-case basis.

The Rights of Job Applicants with Epilepsy

The ADA limits the medical information that an employer can seek from a job applicant. An employer may not ask questions about an applicant's medical condition or require an applicant to take a medical examination before it makes a conditional job offer. This means that an employer *cannot* ask an applicant questions such as:

- whether she has epilepsy or seizures;
- whether she uses any prescription drugs; or
- whether she ever has filed for workers' compensation or was injured on a job.

After making a job offer, an employer may ask questions about an applicant's health and may require a medical examination as long as it treats all applicants the same.

Does the ADA require an applicant to disclose that she has epilepsy or some other disability before accepting a job offer?

No, the ADA does not require applicants to disclose that they have epilepsy or another disability unless they will need a reasonable accommodation for the application process. Some individuals with epilepsy, however, choose to disclose their condition to eliminate any surprise should a seizure occur in the workplace. Often the

The U.S. Population Distribution of Various Disabilities

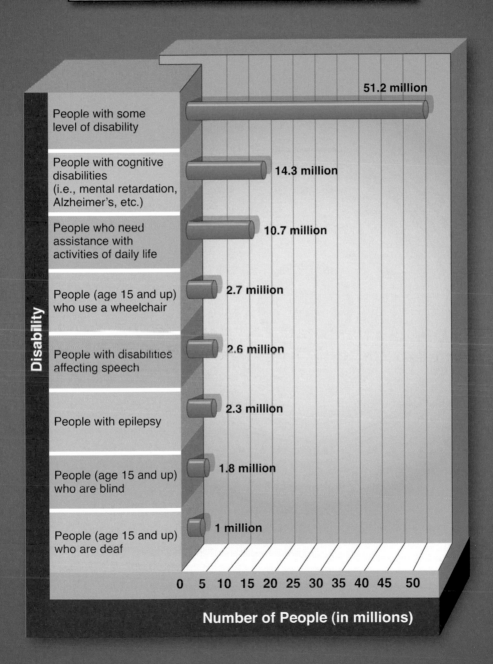

Disability

Disability	Number of People (in millions)
People with some level of disability	51.2 million
People with cognitive disabilities (i.e., mental retardation, Alzheimer's, etc.)	14.3 million
People who need assistance with activities of daily life	10.7 million
People (age 15 and up) who use a wheelchair	2.7 million
People with disabilities affecting speech	2.6 million
People with epilepsy	2.3 million
People (age 15 and up) who are blind	1.8 million
People (age 15 and up) who are deaf	1 million

0 5 10 15 20 25 30 35 40 45 50

Number of People (in millions)

Taken from: U.S. Census Bureau, November 17, 2008.

decision to disclose depends on the type of seizure a person has, the need for assistance during or after a seizure, the frequency of seizures, and the type of work for which the person is applying.

Sometimes the decision to disclose depends on whether an individual will need a reasonable accommodation to perform the job. A person with epilepsy, however, may request an accommodation after becoming an employee even if she did not ask for one when applying for the job or after receiving the job offer.

May an employer ask any follow-up questions if an applicant voluntarily reveals that she has epilepsy?

If an applicant voluntarily discloses that she has epilepsy, an employer only may ask two questions: whether she needs a reasonable accommodation, and if so, what type. The employer also must keep any information an applicant discloses about her medical condition confidential.

Example: An individual applies for a data clerk position. She tells the interviewer that she does not have a driver's license due to epilepsy and will need a flexible schedule because public transportation is not always reliable. She also mentions that she has not had a seizure in more than six months. The interviewer may ask the applicant additional questions about her requested accommodation, such as how early she can start to work and how many hours she can work each day, but cannot ask for details about her epilepsy, such as how long she has had epilepsy or whether she has had to miss work in the past because of her condition.

What should an employer do when it learns that an applicant has epilepsy after he has been offered a job?

FAST FACT

For an employer to refuse to hire a person because of epilepsy is against the law, except for extraordinary cases in which seizures would interfere with the person's ability to safely perform job duties.

The fact that an applicant has epilepsy may not be used to withdraw a job offer if the applicant is able to perform the fundamental duties ("essential functions") of a job, with or without reasonable accommodation, without posing a direct threat to safety. The employer, therefore, should evaluate the applicant's present ability to perform the job effectively and safely. After an offer has been made, an employer also may ask the applicant additional questions about his epilepsy, such as whether he takes any medication; whether he still has seizures and, if so, what type; how long it takes him to recover after a seizure; and/or, whether he will need assistance if he has a seizure at work.

The employer also could send the applicant for a follow-up medical examination or ask him to submit documentation from his doctor answering questions specifically designed to assess the applicant's ability to perform the job's functions and to do so safely.

> *Example*: An experienced chef gets an offer from a hotel resort. During the post-offer medical examination, he discloses that he has had epilepsy for ten years. When the doctor expresses concern about the applicant's ability to work around stoves and use sharp utensils, the applicant explains that his seizures are controlled by medication and offers to bring information from his neurologist to answer the doctor's concerns. He also points out that he has worked as a chef for seven years without incident. Because there is no evidence that the applicant will pose a significant risk of substantial harm while performing the duties of a chef, the employer may not withdraw the job offer.

The Rights of Employees with Epilepsy

When may an employer ask an employee if epilepsy, or some other medical condition, may be affecting her ability to do her job?

An employer may ask questions or require an employee to have a medical examination only when it has a legitimate reason to believe that epilepsy, or some other medical condition, may be affecting the employee's ability to do her job, or to do it safely.

Example: Several times during the past three months, a supervisor has observed a newly hired secretary staring blankly, making chewing movements with her mouth, and engaging in random activity. On these occasions, the secretary has appeared to be unaware of people around her and has not responded when the supervisor has asked if she was okay. The secretary has no memory of these incidents. She also has seemed confused when the supervisor asked her to make corrections on documents she (the secretary) recently typed. The supervisor may ask the secretary whether a medical condition, such as epilepsy, is affecting her ability to perform the essential functions of her job.

On the other hand, when an employer does not have a reason to believe that a medical condition is causing an employee's poor job performance, it may not ask for medical information but should handle the matter as a performance problem.

Example: Lately, a normally reliable receptionist with epilepsy has been missing work on Mondays and leaving work early on Fridays. The supervisor noticed these changes soon after the receptionist's fiancé moved to another state. The supervisor can ask the receptionist about her attendance problems but may not ask her about her epilepsy.

An employer also may ask an employee about epilepsy when it has a reason to believe that the employee may pose a "direct threat" (i.e., a significant risk of substantial harm) to himself or others. An employer should make sure that its safety concerns are based on objective evidence and not general assumptions.

Example: A line cook with epilepsy had three seizures in his first six weeks on the job. Although the cook did not injure himself or anyone else during his seizures, the employer may send him for a medical examination or ask him to submit documentation from his doctor indicating that he can safely perform his job, which requires him to work around flat top grills, hot ovens, and fryers with boiling oil. . . .

Keeping Medical Information Confidential

With limited exceptions, an employer must keep confidential any medical information it learns about an applicant or employee. An employer, however, under certain circumstances may disclose to particular individuals that an employee has epilepsy:

- to supervisors and managers, if necessary to provide a reasonable accommodation or meet an employee's work restrictions;
- to first aid and safety personnel if an employee would need emergency treatment or require some other assistance if she had a seizure at work;
- to individuals investigating compliance with the ADA and similar state and local laws; and,
- as needed for workers' compensation or insurance purposes (for example, to process a claim).

May an employer explain to other employees that their co-worker is allowed to do something that generally is not permitted (such as have more breaks) because he has epilepsy?

No. An employer may not disclose that an employee has epilepsy or is receiving a reasonable accommodation. However, an employer certainly may respond to a question about why a co-worker is receiving what is perceived

On July 26, 1990, President George H.W. Bush signed into law the Americans with Disabilities Act, which made it illegal to discriminate against people with disabilities. (AP Images)

as "different" or "special" treatment by emphasizing that it tries to assist any employee who experiences difficulties in the workplace. The employer also may find it helpful to point out that many of the workplace issues encountered by employees are personal and it is the employer's policy to respect employee privacy.

If an employee has a seizure at work, may an employer explain to other employees or managers that the employee has epilepsy?

No. Although the employee's co-workers and others in the workplace who witness the seizure naturally may be concerned, an employer may not reveal that the employee has epilepsy. Rather, the employer should assure everyone present that the situation is under control. The employer also should follow the employee's plan of action if one has been created.

Example: During a staff meeting, an attorney's arm and leg suddenly start jerking. Although she appears awake, she does not say anything. When another employee asks whether he should call an ambulance, a manager calmly explains that no first aid is necessary and that the attorney will be okay in a few minutes. He adjourns the meeting and stays with the attorney until she recovers from her seizure.

An employer also may allow an employee voluntarily to tell her co-workers that she has epilepsy and provide them with helpful information, such as how to recognize when she is having a seizure, how long her seizures generally last, what, if anything, should be done if she has a seizure, and how long it generally takes her to recover. However, even if an employee voluntarily discloses that she has epilepsy, an employer is limited in sharing this information with others.

Accommodating Employees with Epilepsy
The ADA requires employers to provide adjustments or modifications to enable people with disabilities to enjoy equal employment opportunities unless doing so would be an undue hardship (i.e., a significant difficulty or expense). Accommodations vary depending on the needs of an individual with a disability. Not all employees with epilepsy will need an accommodation or require the same accommodation, and most of the accommodations a person with epilepsy might need will involve little or no cost.

What types of reasonable accommodations may employees with epilepsy need?

Some employees may need one or more of the following accommodations:

- breaks to take medication
- leave to seek treatment or adjust to medication

- a private area to rest after having a seizure
- a rubber mat or carpet to cushion a fall
- adjustments to work schedules

Example: A library schedules employees to work eight-hour shifts starting as early as 8:00 a.m. and as late as 1:00 p.m. A librarian who has epilepsy and experiences nocturnal seizures, which leave her tired in the early morning, requests that her shifts start in the late morning or early afternoon. The employer determines that because there are a sufficient number of staff available between 8:00 a.m. and 10:00 a.m. to respond to requests from the public for assistance, the accommodation can be granted without undue hardship.

- a consistent start time or a schedule change (e.g., from the night shift to the day shift)

Example: A home nurse rotated from working the 7:00 a.m. to 3:00 p.m. shift to the midnight to 8:00 a.m. shift. His doctor wrote a note to the employment agency indicating that interferences in the nurse's sleep were making it difficult for him to get enough rest and, as a result, he was beginning to have more frequent seizures. If eliminating the nurse's midnight rotation would not cause an undue hardship, this would be a reasonable accommodation.

- a checklist to assist in remembering tasks

Example: A box packer would have absence seizures while packing boxes and forget what he was doing. The supervisor created a checklist for each step of the job. Now, when the box packer has a seizure, he simply looks at the checklist to see what steps he has completed.

Other employees with epilepsy may need:

- to bring a service animal to work

- someone to drive to meetings and other work-related events
- to work at home

Example: When a medical transcriber started having frequent, unpredictable seizures at work, she asked her supervisor if she could work at home until her seizures were controlled. Because the transcriber can do the essential functions of her job at home without day-to-day supervision, the employer granted her request.

Although these are some examples of the types of accommodations employees with epilepsy commonly need, other employees may need different changes or adjustments. An employer should ask the employee requesting an accommodation because of his epilepsy what is needed to do the job. There also are extensive public and private resources to help employers identify reasonable accommodations. . . .

Does an employer ever have to reassign an employee with epilepsy to another position?

Yes, reassignment may be necessary where an employee with epilepsy no longer can perform his job, with or without reasonable accommodation, unless the employer can show that it would be an undue hardship. The new position should be equal in pay and status to the employee's original position, or as close as possible if no equivalent position is available. The new position does not have to be a promotion, although the employee should have the right to compete for promotions just like other employees.

Example: A telephone repairman submits a note from his doctor stating that he recently has been diagnosed with epilepsy and must avoid climbing and working at heights above ground level. Although the employer would not have to "bump" another employee from a position to create a vacancy, the employer should determine whether there is another position for which the repairman is qualified that will meet his restrictions.

Requests for Reasonable Accommodation

How does an employee with epilepsy request a reasonable accommodation?

There are no "magic words" that a person has to use when requesting a reasonable accommodation. A person simply has to tell the employer that she needs an adjustment or change at work because of her epilepsy.

> *Example*: A teacher tells her principal that she recently has been diagnosed with epilepsy and needs three weeks off to find out whether medication will control her seizures. This is a request for reasonable accommodation.

A request for reasonable accommodation also can come from a family member, friend, health professional, or other representative on behalf of a person with epilepsy. If the employer does not already know that an employee has epilepsy, the employer can ask the employee for verification from a health care professional.

Does an employer have to grant every request for a reasonable accommodation?

No. An employer does not have to provide an accommodation if doing so will be an undue hardship. Undue hardship means that providing the reasonable accommodation would result in significant difficulty or expense. If a requested accommodation is too difficult or expensive, an employer still would need to determine whether there is another easier or less costly accommodation that would meet the employee's needs.

Is it a reasonable accommodation for an employer to make sure that an employee takes antiseizure medicine as prescribed?

No. Employers have no obligation to monitor an employee to make sure that she does not have a seizure. However, an employer may have to provide a flexible work schedule or allow the employee breaks to rest or to take medication to keep her epilepsy under control.

If an employee does not have a license because of epilepsy, does an employer have to eliminate driving from his job duties?

If driving is an essential function of a job, an employer does not have to eliminate it. However, an employer should carefully consider whether driving actually is a job function or simply a way of accomplishing an essential function. If an accommodation is available that would enable an employee with epilepsy to perform a function that most employees would perform by driving, then the employer must provide the accommodation, absent undue hardship.

> *Example*: A qualified sales clerk applies for promotion to assistant manager of a store. The employer promotes someone else because it claims that an essential function of the assistant manager's job is driving store receipts to the bank. Because *depositing* the receipts in a safe and timely manner, not driving, is the actual function of the job, the employer should have determined whether the sales clerk could have done the job with a reasonable accommodation (e.g., having another employee drive her or paying for her to take a taxi).

Similarly, if driving is a marginal (or non-essential) function, the fact that an individual with epilepsy does not have a driver's license cannot be used to deny the individual an employment opportunity.

> *Example*: College orientation guides are hired to hand out information packets and give tours of the campus. Occasionally, a guide also may be asked to drive prospective students to and from the airport. Not every guide is asked to perform this function,

and there are always other guides available to perform the function if a particular individual is unavailable. Because driving is not an essential function of the job, the college cannot refuse to hire a person to be a guide who does not have a driver's license because of epilepsy but, rather, would have to assign someone else to perform that task.

Concerns About Safety

When it comes to safety, an employer should be careful not to act on the basis of myths, fears, generalizations, or stereotypes about epilepsy. Instead, the employer should evaluate each individual on his knowledge, skills, experience, and how having epilepsy affects him. In other words, an employer should determine whether a *specific* applicant or employee would pose a "direct threat" or significant risk of substantial harm to himself or others that cannot be eliminated or reduced through reasonable accommodation. This assessment must be based on objective, factual evidence, including the best recent medical evidence and advances to treat and control epilepsy.

When may an employer prohibit a person who has epilepsy from performing a job because of safety concerns?

An employer may prohibit a person who has epilepsy from performing a job when it can show that the individual may pose a direct threat. In making a "direct threat" assessment, the employer must evaluate the individual's present ability to safely perform the job. The employer also should consider: (1) the duration of the risk; (2) the nature and severity of the potential harm; (3) the likelihood that the potential harm will occur; and, (4) the imminence of the potential harm. The harm also must be serious and likely to occur, not remote and speculative. Finally, the employer must determine whether any reasonable accommodation would reduce or eliminate the risk.

Example: A tool inspector with epilepsy applies to be a welder for the same company. During the past two years, the employee has on several occasions failed to take prescribed medication and has experienced sudden and unpredictable seizures at work. Because of the likelihood that the employee would experience sudden and unpredictable seizures and the serious consequences that would result if the employee had a seizure while working as a welder, the employer may deny the employee the job.

What should an employer do when another federal law prohibits it from hiring anyone who has epilepsy?

The employer has a defense to a charge of discrimination under the ADA if a federal law prohibits it from hiring a person with epilepsy. The employer should be certain, however, that compliance with the law actually is *required*, not voluntary and that the law does not contain any exceptions or waivers.

Employers Should Take Actions Against Harassment

Employers are prohibited from harassing or allowing employees with disabilities to be harassed in the workplace. When harassment is brought to the attention of a supervisor, the supervisor must take steps to stop it.

What should employers do to prevent and correct harassment?

Employers should make clear that they will not tolerate harassment based on disability or on any other basis (i.e., race, sex, religion, national origin, or age). This can be done in a number of ways, such as through a written policy, employee handbooks, staff meetings, and periodic training. The employer should emphasize that harassment is prohibited and that employees should promptly report such conduct to a manager. Finally, the employer should immediately conduct a thorough investigation of any report of harassment and take swift and appropriate corrective action.

CHAPTER 3

Living with Epilepsy

Unraveling the Secret of the Spells

Christine Contillo

In the following article Christine Contillo recounts how she discovered that the occasional fainting spells she had experienced since childhood were actually a mild form of epilepsy. She admits that she is embarrassed to tell others about her condition, though it is well controlled with medication, and notes that in America, a taboo still exists against those who have mental illnesses or neurological disorders. Contillo is a supervising public health nurse who resides in Paramus, New Jersey.

Ten years ago I was on vacation, sitting at a harborside restaurant in Baltimore sipping a daiquiri. We had planned to leave the next morning on a daylong Chesapeake Bay cruise. With that drink my whole world, and my perception of myself in it, changed.

As I watched my husband point to a boat bobbing in the sunset, I realized that something felt wrong. I'd had this feeling before. I was lightheaded, but somehow

Photo on facing page. Baltimore Ravens cornerback Samari Rolle (22) has epilepsy and has had an outstanding pro football career. (Mark Goldman/UPI/Landov)

SOURCE: Christine Contillo, "Unraveling the Secret of the Spells," *The New York Times*, November 18, 2003, p. F5. Copyright © 2003 by The New York Times Company. Reproduced by permission.

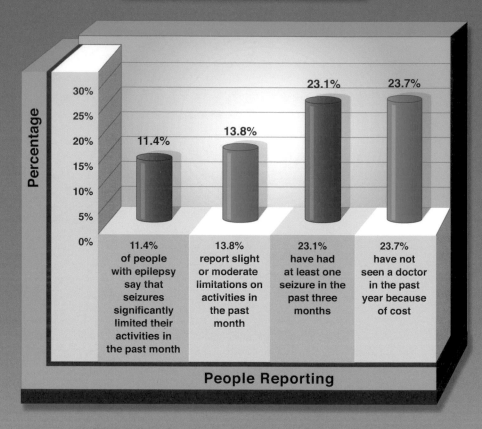

Coping with Seizures

Percentage (y-axis)

30%
25%
20%
15%
10%
5%
0%

11.4%	13.8%	23.1%	23.7%
11.4% of people with epilepsy say that seizures significantly limited their activities in the past month	13.8% report slight or moderate limitations on activities in the past month	23.1% have had at least one seizure in the past three months	23.7% have not seen a doctor in the past year because of cost

People Reporting (x-axis)

Taken from: Victoria Stagg Elliott, *American Medical News*, September 8, 2008.

that wasn't all. The lights were too bright, the colors too vibrant, the sounds too loud, and it seemed as if time was moving too slow. I could follow the conversation but couldn't join in. That's what I remember before my head hit the table.

A Trip to the Emergency Room

What followed was an ambulance ride to the hospital, where I was admitted through the E.R. A cardiac event was quickly ruled out, but because I'd had a previous head injury the admitting doctor called for a neurologist and left.

A first-year resident arrived, and fired a battery of questions at me. I said I'd been having these spells since I was about 10, once or twice a year, but that they'd always been largely shrugged off. I described a head injury in my teens which had never caused me any trouble. He left. Time ticked on.

The chief neurology resident came in, asked more of the same questions, and they left together. After midnight they were back again, explaining that this might be something serious and were about to call in the attending physician. I'm a nurse: I know that you had better have a good reason for calling in the senior statesman in the middle of the night.

He arrived, gently told me that it could be a brain lesion or an undetected serious infection and asked for permission to run additional and costly tests, which were completed by dawn.

They didn't find much and discharged me with a handshake, a joke about staying away from daiquiris and a promise that I would follow up with my own doctor. He listened to the story and sent me off to a cardiologist. That visit turned up nothing and was in turn followed by a visit with another neurologist. After reading through the notes, the neurologist admonished me that nothing would be gained by pursuing this further if these spells happened so rarely.

But then, a month later, the original first-year neurology resident from Baltimore called. A bulldog of a diagnostician, he told me that he'd looked over my chart and the test results again, come up with a new plan and wanted to speak to my local neurologist.

I gave him the phone number, new tests were run, and, it seems, I have a mild form of epilepsy. My fainting spells were really seizures. I was put on medication and did well. Thus my driver's license stayed intact, and I no longer worry that I'll lose consciousness unexpectedly.

> **FAST FACT**
>
> Many celebrities with epilepsy fear that going public with their disorder will result in negative treatment and harm their employment opportunities.

Embarrassed to Tell Others

Something about this has always bothered me, though. I was supposed to meet my cousin for breakfast in Baltimore that morning long ago, but had to break the date because of my brief hospitalization.

I was a little embarrassed to tell her about my illness, but surprisingly she volunteered that her daughter had

The author relates her experiences of fainting spells early in her childhood that were a mild form of epilepsy not easily diagnosed. (AJPhoto/ Photo Researchers, Inc.)

the same symptoms and was also taking medication. In 20 years, she had shared this with very few people, and no one in our family. I realized that we'll tell neighbors about failed marriages or addictions and bare our breast reconstructions to strangers in therapy groups, but in America we keep mental and emotional illness and neurological problems very close to the vest.

In the Hmong culture of Cambodia, epilepsy is considered good fortune. The soul leaves the body, the tradition holds, and goes exploring during a seizure. We just find it messy. We look the other way when we see people suffering from illness above the shoulders, as if even acknowledging it could jinx our own family.

And why had doctors always been so willing to toss off my symptoms? I think I always wondered what was wrong. We'd told my pediatrician, obstetrician and internist, but they'd explained it away by giving a host of excuses: it was too hot out, I'd sat up too fast, it was just hormones or I'd run too far.

In truth, it probably just wasn't interesting enough.

We value the seasoned physician with the large practice and lots of experience, but it took the doctor in training with something to prove to diagnose this disorder. Because he was puzzled and thorough, I'll never have to wonder what might have happened the next time. I hope the patients he has had since have looked past his boyish face and can appreciate the fine doctor that I'm sure he's become.

What I Hate the Most Is Losing My Memory

John Flynn

John Flynn suffered his first seizure more than two decades ago after experiencing a "dreamy feeling," or aura, while on a walk near his home. He was diagnosed with complex partial epilepsy, in which one senses that a seizure is about to happen, then "comes to" after several minutes, with no memory of what ensued during that time. This loss of memory is what Flynn finds most frustrating about his disorder. He is also distressed when he is treated impersonally by medical personnel, but he has found support and reassurance by joining an epilepsy support group. Flynn works at Bangor University and lives in Caernarfon, Wales.

I have always been a very active sort of person, running marathons and playing squash. The first time I had an attack of epilepsy was 25 years ago. It was a shock to me.

SOURCE: John Flynn, "Epilepsy Is a Taboo but Now I Have Confidence to Open Up to Anyone About the Condition," *Western Mail* (Cardiff, Wales), October 6, 2008, p. 24. Coyright © 2008 Western Mail and Echo Ltd. All rights reserved. Reproduced by permission.

It was weird—I was walking along the road from my house to my dad's, when I had a dreamy feeling. The next thing everything was blank. I came around about 10 minutes later in front of my own house.

I went to my doctor immediately—I was scared stiff as I thought I was losing my mind. But after talking to the doctor he told me the only thing that could have caused an attack of epilepsy could have been a head trauma.

The only thing I could remember was that a week before a lad hit me and I passed out, knocking my head on the road.

The doctor referred me to the local hospital, which then referred me to the Walton Centre, in Liverpool. It ran tests—including an EEG and MRI scan [tests to monitor functions and electrical activity of the brain]—and the results showed I had a scarring on the temporal lobe section of the brain.

They told me it could have been the punch that caused this, but by looking at my notes they saw that I had meningitis when I was six years old.

> **FAST FACT**
>
> A preseizure aura may include symptoms such as lightheadedness, dizziness, and oversensitivity to light or sound.

Medication and Other Support

For the next month or so I was in a daze. I was put on the drug Tegretol—like most medications there were side-effects. I felt like a zombie, I was lethargic and not scared of anything. I had to take it three times a day.

Eventually I contacted an epilepsy support group. The atmosphere here was like a family, they also confided in me and they reassured me.

My type of epilepsy is complex partial. I always get an aura (warning) and the next thing I'm on auto pilot. Ten minutes can pass, I can enter the house, lock the doors and phone my wife.

The next thing I come around panicking with no memory of where I am and what day it is. This can last for about five to 10 minutes and then everything comes

The author relates his experiences of partial epilepsy seizures that leave no memory of what has happened during that time.
(© Urban Zone/Alamy)

flooding back. The worst thing about epilepsy for me is this problem with my memory.

At the time of the diagnosis I was shocked about the clinical approach towards epilepsy—did they know how scared I was? It felt to me like there was no emotion. Still, to this day, I come across newly diagnosed patients who have just been sent home with a leaflet about epilepsy.

Now, because of my confidence, I open up to anybody and listen to their problems and try to help as much as I can.

I joined a forum on Epilepsy Action—this was the best thing I did, as it answered all the questions, from a patient's perspective, rather than a doctor's.

Every time I see my neurologist I feel as though I am not a person. It seems as though he is looking at my brain and not at me. The best person I have come across is the epilepsy specialist nurse.

Reaching Out to Others

About four years ago I became a tutor for the expert patient programme—this helped me a lot. It was run over six weeks. We were asked to write down our worries and pass them to the person next to you. We had to stand up and read each of our stories out—the person next to me reading my story started to cry. The person had arthritis and couldn't walk far. They told me that they wouldn't like to lose their memory.

We both cried and I explained that I was fit and healthy and could run. This showed me everybody looks at life in a different way.

Epilepsy to this day is still a taboo subject and the most helpful person I've come across is the specialist nurse. She explained everything and always listened and knew when to step in.

To me the personal touch of the treatment meant everything.

Losing Our Daughter to Epilepsy

Jeff Wilson

Jeff Wilson is the father of a teenage girl who tragically died as a result of an epileptic seizure. His daughter Gen began having grand mal seizures at age sixteen, and although she was given medication she continued to suffer seizures in a variety of public and private places. Because so many things can trigger seizures, they can be very unpredictable—making even ordinary activities potentially dangerous for a person with epilepsy. Wilson tells Gen's story with the hope of raising awareness about neurological disorders and the need for epilepsy research.

If you are reading this, it is probably because someone you love suffers from seizures. I am writing this because on June 22, 2007, I lost my beautiful nineteen-year-old daughter Generose as the result of a seizure. I just pray I can reach out and help other families so they do not go through the devastation my family lives through every day. If this helps raise awareness of epilepsy, or raises

SOURCE: Jeff Wilson, "Gen's Story," *Faces of Epilepsy*, 2008. Reproduced by permission.

contributions to further epilepsy research, then my pain is eased a little. It will never go away because the memory of Gen will always be with me.

"Blond Moments"

Gen had been having grand mal seizures since she was about sixteen, although we now suspect she was having seizures before then. She would have a "blond moment," where she would pause for a brief second while talking. This was probably the start of her seizures but we didn't know and thought it was more of a way she gathered attention or played the role of a "blond." We joked about it.

Her friends revealed to us that every once in a while they noticed Gen's eyes roll up and lock for a few seconds. In high school, she "blacked out." The school notified us, and we took her to a neurologist. He told us she was having seizures, and started her on medication right away. Her first big seizure happened at a hockey game and that was the first of about six trips by ambulance to the emergency room over the next two years.

As she experienced more and more seizures, the medications were increased. Getting a teenager to understand the importance of taking medication on a regular schedule seemed impossible. Gen had seizures at her high school, at a restaurant, at her dorm room in college, at home a few times. These are the ones we know about; there's no telling if she had them during the night in bed or other places. We suspect she had one in the bathroom at work, after the prom, and once in a car while waiting for her brother.

FAST FACT

More than 50 million people worldwide have epilepsy.

The Unpredictability of Seizures

It was not until after Gen's death that we realized so many things can spark a seizure—change in temperature, stress, infections, menstrual cycles, hormones, lack of sleep, bright lights . . . the list goes on and on. You can't predict seizures. So do you live in a bubble? Think about it; most normal activities can turn disastrous when a seizure happens. Gen suffered a seizure and drowned while taking a relaxing bath in the garden tub.

Gen was burning the candle at both ends—going to college, working, and living life to the fullest with her enormous group of friends. Gen was definitely the instigator of social activities, and played the role of counselor for the lovelorn. The devastation felt by her family has been equally felt by her friends, who in reality were also her family. We have planted trees at her high school, purchased bracelets and lanyards in her memory, and

A young homeless woman who later died endures an epileptic seizure. The author relates his experience of losing his daughter to epilepsy. (AP Images)

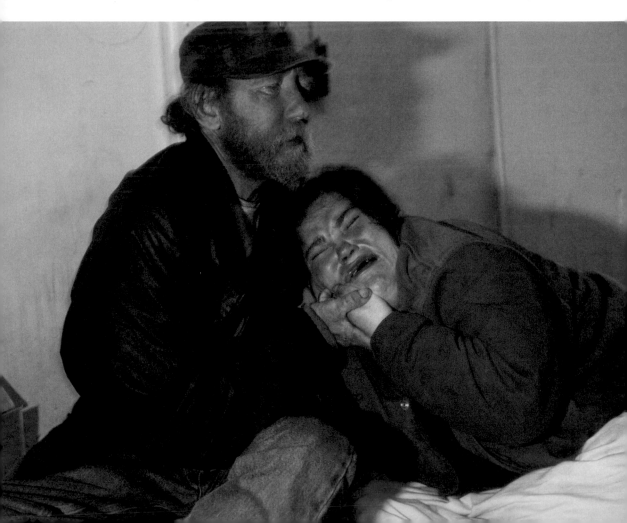

started web sites on Facebook.com in her memory. In death, Gen continues to give; from donated tissue for research, to corneas to give sight to two individuals—even clothes for the less fortunate.

Writing this is not easy. But when I read the facts that the second most common cause of disability or death in children fourteen and younger is seizures, my heart goes out to all that may be faced with the physical, emotional, psychological, and spiritual drain from losing a child. I had to tell Gen's story; that's how she would have done it.

The Life of an Epileptic Autistic Savant

Richard Johnson

In the following selection Richard Johnson profiles the life of Daniel Tammet, an autistic savant who also has epilepsy. Savants are people who have unusual and amazing mental capacities, such as the ability to solve complex math problems in seconds or memorize an entire book after one reading. Tammet suffered his first epileptic seizure at age three, after which he developed a fascination with numbers and counting. Johnson notes that Tammet is also uniquely gifted in language and comprehension—he can speak seven languages and is in the process of creating a new one. This facility with language—an unusual skill for an autistic savant—has made him the focus of international scientific interest. Johnson writes for the *Guardian*, a British newspaper.

D aniel Tammet is talking. As he talks, he studies my shirt and counts the stitches. Ever since the age of three, when he suffered an epileptic fit, Tammet has been obsessed with counting. Now he is 26, and a mathematical genius who can figure out cube roots quicker than a calculator and recall pi to 22,514 decimal places. He also happens to be autistic, which is why he can't drive a car, wire a plug, or tell right from left. He lives with extraordinary ability and disability.

Tammet is calculating 377 multiplied by 795. Actually, he isn't "calculating": there is nothing conscious about what he is doing. He arrives at the answer instantly. Since his epileptic fit, he has been able to see numbers as shapes, colours and textures. The number two, for instance, is a motion, and five is a clap of thunder. "When I multiply numbers together, I see two shapes. The image starts to change and evolve, and a third shape emerges. That's the answer. It's mental imagery. It's like maths without having to think."

Extraordinary Abilities

Tammet is a "savant", an individual with an astonishing, extraordinary mental ability. An estimated 10% of the autistic population—and an estimated 1% of the non-autistic population—have savant abilities, but no one knows exactly why. A number of scientists now hope that Tammet might help us to understand better. Professor Allan Snyder, from the Centre for the Mind at the Australian National University in Canberra, explains why Tammet is of particular, and international, scientific interest. "Savants can't usually tell us how they do what they do," says Snyder. "It just comes to them. Daniel can. He describes what he sees in his head. That's why he's exciting. He could be the Rosetta Stone [an Egyptian artifact used as a tool to understand ancient hieroglyphic writing]."

There are many theories about savants. Snyder, for instance, believes that we all possess the savant's extraordinary abilities—it is just a question of us learning how to access them. "Savants have usually had some kind of brain damage. Whether it's an onset of dementia later in life, a blow to the head or, in the case of Daniel, an epileptic fit. And it's that brain damage which creates the savant. I think that it's possible for a perfectly normal person to have access to these abilities, so working with Daniel could be very instructive."

Scans of the brains of autistic savants suggest that the right hemisphere might be compensating for damage in the left hemisphere. While many savants struggle with language and comprehension (skills associated primarily with the left hemisphere), they often have amazing skills in mathematics and memory (primarily right hemisphere skills). Typically, savants have a limited vocabulary, but there is nothing limited about Tammet's vocabulary.

Amazing Language and Math Skills

Tammet is creating his own language, strongly influenced by the vowel and image-rich languages of northern Europe. (He already speaks French, German, Spanish, Lithuanian, Icelandic and Esperanto.) The vocabulary of his language—"Mänti", meaning a type of tree—reflects the relationships between different things. The word "ema", for instance, translates as "mother", and "ela" is what a mother creates: "life". "Päike" is "sun", and "päive" is what the sun creates: "day". Tammet hopes to launch Mänti in academic circles later this year [2005], his own personal exploration of the power of words and their inter-relationship.

Professor Simon Baron-Cohen, director of the Autism Research Centre (ARC) at Cambridge University, is interested in what Mänti might teach us about savant ability. "I know of other savants who also speak a lot of languages," says Baron-Cohen. "But it's rare for them to be able to reflect on how they do it—let alone create a language of their own." The ARC team has started scanning Tammet's brain to find out if there are modules (for number, for example, or for colour, or for texture) that are connected in a way that is different from most of us. "It's too early to tell, but we hope it might throw some light on why we don't all have savant abilities."

[In 2004] Tammet broke the European record for recalling pi, the mathematical constant, to the furthest decimal point. He found it easy, he says, because he didn't even have to "think". To him, pi isn't an abstract set of digits; it's a visual story, a film projected in front of his eyes. He learnt the number forwards and backwards and, last year, spent five hours recalling it in front of an adjudicator. He wanted to prove a point. "I memorised pi to 22,514 decimal places, and I am technically disabled. I just wanted to show people that disability needn't get in the way."

> **FAST FACT**
>
> Epilepsy occurs at a 15 percent higher rate among people with autism.

A Sense of Control

Tammet is softly spoken, and shy about making eye contact, which makes him seem younger than he is. He lives on the Kent coast, but never goes near the beach—there are too many pebbles to count. The thought of a mathematical problem with no solution makes him feel uncomfortable. Trips to the supermarket are always a chore. "There's too much mental stimulus. I have to look at every shape and texture. Every price, and every arrangement of fruit and vegetables. So instead of thinking, 'What cheese do I want this week?', I'm just really uncomfortable."

Tammet has never been able to work 9 to 5. It would be too difficult to fit around his daily routine. For instance, he has to drink his cups of tea at exactly the same time every day. Things have to happen in the same order: he always brushes his teeth before he has his shower. "I have tried to be more flexible, but I always end up feeling more uncomfortable. Retaining a sense of control is really important. I like to do things in my own time, and in my own style, so an office with targets and bureaucracy just wouldn't work."

Instead, he has set up a business on his own, at home, writing email courses in language learning, numeracy and literacy for private clients. It has had the fringe benefit of keeping human interaction to a minimum. It also gives him time to work on the verb structures of Mänti.

Meeting Rain Man

Few people on the streets have recognised Tammet since his pi record attempt. But, when a documentary about his life is broadcast on Channel 5 later [in 2005], all that will change. "The highlight of filming was to meet Kim Peek, the real-life character who inspired the film *Rain Man*. Before I watched *Rain Man*, I was frightened. As a nine-year-old schoolboy, you don't want people to point at the screen and say, 'That's you.' But I watched it, and felt a real connection. Getting to meet the real-life Rain Man was inspirational."

Peek was shy and introspective, but he sat and held Tammet's hand for hours. "We shared so much—our love of key dates from history, for instance. And our love of books. As a child, I regularly took over a room in the house and started my own lending library. I would separate out fiction and non-fiction, and then alphabetise them all. I even introduced a ticketing system. I love books so much. I've read more books than anyone else I know. So I was delighted when Kim wanted to meet in a library." Peek can read two pages simultaneously, one with each eye. He can also recall, in exact detail, the 7,600 books he has read. When he is at home in Utah, he spends afternoons at the Salt Lake City public library, memorising phone books and address directories. "He is such a lovely man," says Tammet. "Kim says, 'You don't have to be handicapped to be different—everybody's different'. And he's right."

Like Peek, Tammet will read anything and everything, but his favourite book is a good dictionary, or the works of GK Chesterton [an early 20th-century writer nicknamed "the prince of paradox"]. "With all those aphorisms," he says, "Chesterton was the Groucho Marx of his day." Tammet is also a Christian, and likes the fact that Chesterton addressed some complex religious ideas. "The other thing I like is that, judging by the descriptions of his home life, I reckon Chesterton was a savant. He couldn't dress himself, and would always forget where he was going. His poor wife."

Autistic savants have displayed a wide range of talents, from reciting all nine volumes of *Grove's Dictionary Of Music* to measuring exact distances with the naked eye. The blind American savant Leslie Lemke played [Russian composer Pyotr Ilyich] Tchaikovsky's Piano Concerto No 1, after he heard it for the first time, and he never had so much as a piano lesson. And the British savant Stephen Wiltshire was able to draw a highly accurate map of the London skyline from memory after a single helicopter trip over the city. Even so, Tammet could still turn out to be the more significant.

Tammet's Early Years

He was born on January 31 1979. He smiles as he points out that 31, 19, 79 and 1979 are all prime numbers—it's a kind of sign. He was actually born with another surname, which he prefers to keep private, but decided to change it by deed poll [i.e., legally]. It didn't fit with the way he saw himself. "I first saw 'Tammet' online. It means oak tree in Estonian, and I liked that association. Besides, I've always had a love of Estonian. Such a vowel rich language."

As a baby, he banged his head against the wall and cried constantly. Nobody knew what was wrong. His mother was anxious, and would swing him to sleep in a blanket. She breastfed him for two years. The only thing the doctors could say was that perhaps he was under-stimulated. Then, one afternoon when he was playing with his brother in the living room, he had an epileptic fit.

"I was given medication—round blue tablets—to control my seizures, and told not to go out in direct sunlight. I had to visit the hospital every month for regular

Daniel Tammet, a British high-functioning autistic savant, is a gifted mathematician and linguist. He has authored two books. (Gerard Julien/AFP/Getty Images)

blood tests. I hated those tests, but I knew they were necessary. To make up for it, my father would always buy me a cup of squash [sweetened citrus juice with soda water] to drink while we sat in the waiting room. It was a worrying time because my Dad's father had epilepsy, and actually died of it, in the end. They were thinking, 'This is the end of Daniel's life'."

Tammet's mother was a secretarial assistant, and his father a steelplate worker. "They both left school without qualifications, but they made us feel special—all nine of us. As the oldest of nine, I suppose it's fair to say I've always felt special." Even if his younger brothers and sisters could throw and catch better than him, swim better, kick a ball better, Daniel was always the oldest. "They loved me because I was their big brother and I could read them stories."

He remembers being given a Ladybird book called *Counting* when he was four. "When I looked at the numbers I 'saw' images. It felt like a place I could go where I really belonged. That was great. I went to this other country whenever I could. I would sit on the floor in my bedroom and just count. I didn't notice that time was passing. It was only when my Mum shouted up for dinner, or someone knocked at my door, that I would snap out of it."

One day his brother asked him a sum. "He asked me to multiply something in my head—like 'What is 82 x 82 x 82 x 82?' I just looked at the floor and closed my eyes. My back went very straight and I made my hands into fists. But after five or 10 seconds, the answer just flowed out of my mouth. He asked me several others, and I got every one right. My parents didn't seem surprised. And they never put pressure on me to perform for the neighbours. They knew I was different, but wanted me to have a normal life as far as possible."

Tammet could see the car park of his infant school from his bedroom window, which made him feel safe. "I loved assembly because we got to sing hymns. The notes formed a pattern in my head, just like the numbers did." The other children didn't know what to make of him, and would tease him. The minute the bell went for playtime he would rush off. "I went to the playground, but not to play. The place was surrounded by trees. While the other children were playing football, I would just stand and count the leaves."

Adolescence and Early Adulthood

As Tammet grew older, he developed an obsessive need to collect—everything from conkers [chestnuts] to newspapers. "I remember seeing a ladybird for the first time," he says. "I loved it so much, I went round searching every hedge and every leaf for more. I collected hundreds, and took them to show the teacher. He was amazed, and asked me to get on with some assignment. While I was busy he instructed a classmate to take the tub outside and let the ladybirds go. I was so upset that I cried when I found out. He didn't understand my world."

Tammet may have been teased at school, but his teachers were always protective. "I think my parents must have had a word with them, so I was pretty much left alone." He found it hard to socialise with anyone outside the family, and, with the advent of adolesence, his shyness got worse.

After leaving school with three A-levels (History, French and German, all grade Bs), he decided he wanted to teach—only not the predictable, learn-by-rote type of teaching. For a start, he went to teach in Lithuania, and he worked as a volunteer. "Because I was there of my own free will, I was given a lot of leeway. The times of the classes weren't set in stone, and the structures were all of my own making. It was also the first time I was introduced as 'Daniel' rather than 'the guy who can do weird stuff in his head'. It was such a pleasant relief." Later, he returned home to live with his parents, and found work as a maths tutor.

He met the great love of his life, a software engineer called Neil, online. It began, as these things do, with emailed pictures, but ended up with a face-to-face meeting. "Because I can't drive, Neil offered to pick me up at my parents' house, and drive me back to his house in Kent. He was silent all the way back. I thought, 'Oh dear, this isn't going well'. Just before we got to his house, he stopped the car. He reached over and pulled out a bouquet of flowers. I only found out later that he was quiet because he likes to concentrate when he's driving."

Neil is shy, like Tammet. They live, happily, on a quiet cul-de-sac. The only aspect of Tammet's autism that causes them problems is his lack of empathy. "There's a saying in Judaism, if somebody has a relative who has hanged themselves, don't ask them where you should hang your coat. I need to remember that. Like the time I kept quizzing a friend of Neil's who had just lost her mother. I was asking her all these questions about faith and death. But that's down to my condition—no taboos."

When he isn't working, Tammet likes to hang out with his friends on the church quiz team. His knowledge of popular culture lets him down, but he's a shoo-in when it comes to the maths questions. "I do love numbers," he says. "It isn't only an intellectual or aloof thing that I do. I really feel that there is an emotional attachment, a caring for numbers. I think this is a human thing—in the same way that a poet humanises a river or a tree through metaphor, my world gives me a sense of numbers as personal. It sounds silly, but numbers are my friends."

GLOSSARY

absence seizure	A generalized seizure involving a lapse of consciousness with a blank stare, usually lasting twenty seconds or less. May include rapid eye blinking or chewing motions. More common in children. Also known as petit mal seizure.
AED (antiepileptic drug)	A medication that prevents seizures.
Americans with Disabilities Act	A law that makes discrimination against people with disabilities illegal; the act applies to employment and access to public places.
atonic seizure	A generalized seizure in which a complete loss of muscle control and balance causes collapse.
aura	A sensation that signals the onset of a seizure, such as dizziness, uneasiness, or visual and other sensory illusions.
bioavailability	The amount of a drug in a pill that the body metabolizes.
brand-name drug	Medication manufactured by a major pharmaceutical company; these tend to be more expensive than generic drugs, but some assert that brand-name drugs are more uniform in the amount of drug and method of preparation.
CAT (computed axial tomography) scan	An imaging technique that creates three-dimensional pictures of the brain, showing possible abnormalities.
cerebral hemisphere	One side of the cerebrum (upper brain). Each hemisphere contains four lobes: frontal, parietal, occipital, and temporal.
clonic	A seizure that involves muscle contractions and relaxations on both sides of the body.
cognition	Pertaining to the mental processes of thinking, perceiving, learning, and remembering.

controlled study	An experiment in which two groups are the same except one group receives the treatment being tested, the other does not.
convulsion	Involuntary muscle contraction common in generalized tonic-clonic seizures.
corpus callosotomy	Surgery that disconnects the cerebral hemispheres. Effective in reducing atonic and tonic-clonic seizures.
EEG (electro-encephalograph)	A machine used for the recording of brain waves through electrodes attached to the scalp.
epilepsy	Chronic neurological disorder characterized by recurrent seizures.
focal seizure	An epileptic seizure that involves one hemisphere of the brain. Also known as partial seizure.
generalized seizure	An epileptic seizure that involves the whole brain.
generic drug	A medication not sold under a brand name. Tends to be less expensive than a brand-name drug, but some assert that generic drugs are less uniform in quality.
grand mal seizure	*See* tonic-clonic seizure.
idiopathic epilepsy	A form of epilepsy of which the cause is unknown.
intractable	Not responding to treatment.
ketogenic diet	A high-fat, high-protein, low-carbohydrate diet that controls seizures in some children.
monotherapy	Treatment with a single drug.
MRI (magnetic resonance imaging)	An imaging method that uses magnets instead of X-rays. It produces detailed pictures of the interior of the body or the brain.
neuron	Nerve cell.
partial seizure	*See* focal seizure.

petit mal seizure	*See* absence seizure.
seizure	Abnormal electrical discharge in the brain. Not always a sign of epilepsy.
simple partial seizure	A seizure in one part of the brain that causes jerking of one area of the body or sensory illusions.
status epilepticus	Severe, potentially life-threatening nonstop seizures that may or may not be related to epilepsy.
TBI (traumatic brain injury)	A severe brain injury, such as one that might result from a car accident or combat wound. TBIs can result in the development of epilepsy years after the event.
tonic-clonic seizure	A generalized seizure that often begins with a fall and muscle rigidity (tonic phase) followed by convulsions, shallow breathing, and possible loss of bladder and bowel control (clonic phase), with ensuing loss of consciousness, confusion, and fatigue. The most noticeable kind of seizure. Also known as grand mal.
vagus nerve	A nerve that originates in the brain stem and reaches to the throat, larynx, lungs, esophagus, heart, and abdomen.
vagus nerve stimulator (VNS)	A pacemaker-like device that minimizes the severity of seizures through electrical stimulation of the vagus nerve.

CHRONOLOGY

B.C.   **400**   Greek physician Hippocrates writes *On the Sacred Disease*, the first book on epilepsy.

A.D.   **1494**   Seizures are described as a characteristic of witches in *Malleus Maleficarum*, a church-authorized witch-hunting handbook.

       1754   Pedro de Horta writes the first epilepsy textbook in the Western Hemisphere.

       1857   The first hospital for "the paralyzed and epileptic" is founded in London.

       1860   Physician Sir John Russell Reynolds challenges the theory that connects epilepsy with mental illness.

       1873   Neurologist John Hughlings Jackson hypothesizes that seizures can be traced to irregular brain activity.

       1881   Neurologist William Gowers classifies seizures as "grand mal," "petit mal," and "hysteroid."

       1886   Neurosurgeon Victor Horsley performs the first successful resection surgery for partial seizures.

       1904   Neurologist William Spratling first coins the term "epileptologist."

1912   Phenobarbital, the first antiepileptic drug (AED), is created.

1921   Physician R.M. Wilder devises the ketogenic diet as a treatment for epilepsy.

1929   German psychiatrist Hans Berger creates the electroencephalograph (EEG).

1939   Dilantin (phenytoin) is introduced as a major nonsedating AED.

1953   Tegretol (carbamazepine) is introduced as an AED.

1954   The American Epilepsy Society is established.

1958   Ethosuximide is introduced as an AED for children with absence seizures.

1964   Paul Zindel's play, *The Effect of Gamma Rays on Man-in-the-Moon Marigolds*, featuring a character with epilepsy, premieres in New York.

1968   The Epilepsy Foundation is established.

1970   A British law forbidding people with epilepsy to marry is repealed.

1970s   The U.S. Veterans Administration spearheads a movement to establish special centers for the treatment of epilepsy.

1980   Positron emission tomography (PET) scan clarifies physiology of epilepsy.

1988   The first vagus nerve stimulator is implanted in a human being.

1990   The U.S. Congress passes the Americans with Disabilities Act, prohibiting discrimination on the basis of disability.

1993–2000   Eight new drugs, including Neurontin, Topamax, and Keppra, are approved for the treatment of epilepsy.

1997   The U.S. Food and Drug Administration (FDA) approves vagus nerve stimulation as a treatment for partial epilepsy in adults.

2000   The Epilepsy Foundation holds a landmark conference, "Curing Epilepsy: The Promise and the Challenge."

2003   Explosive devices used in the wars in Iraq and Afghanistan create a surge in traumatic brain injuries, increasing the potential for epilepsy in combat veterans.

2007   The American Academy of Neurology and others offer congressional testimony in support of increased funding for epilepsy research and treatment.

ORGANIZATIONS TO CONTACT

The editors have compiled the following list of organizations concerned with the issues debated in this book. The descriptions are derived from materials provided by the organizations. All have publications or information available for interested readers. The list was compiled on the date of publication of the present volume; the information provided here may change. Be aware that many organizations take several weeks or longer to respond to inquiries, so allow as much time as possible.

American Academy of Neurology (AAN)
1080 Montreal Ave.
Saint Paul, MN 55116
(800) 879-1960
fax: (651) 695-2791
www.aan.com

Established in 1948, the American Academy of Neurology is an international professional association of more than twenty-one thousand neurologists and neuroscience professionals who care for patients with neurological disorders. Its home page features information on recently developed guidelines on epilepsy and pregnancy as well as links to current science news articles.

American Epilepsy Society (AES)
www.aesnet.org

The AES is a professional society of physicians and scientists who specialize in epileptology, the field of neurology concerned with the study, diagnosis, and treatment of epilepsy. The society promotes research and education for professionals dedicated to the prevention, treatment, and cure of epilepsy. Included at its Web site are links to articles in the *AES Newsletter* and the journals *Epilepsy Currents* and *Epilepsia*.

Canine Assistants
3160 Francis Rd.
Milton, GA 30004
(770) 664-7178
fax: (770) 664-7820
www.canineassistants
.org

Canine Assistants is a nonprofit organization that trains and provides service dogs for children and adults with physical disabilities and other special needs. It also trains seizure response dogs for certain recipients, providing service animals that can remain next to a person during a seizure, summon help, and in some cases predict and react to an oncoming seizure in advance. General information about applying for a Canine Assistants service dog, as well as links to a national volunteer program that provides community education about service dogs, are available at its Web site.

Centers for Disease Control and Prevention (CDC)
1600 Clifton Rd.
Atlanta, GA 30333
(800) 232-4636 or
(888) 232-6348
www.cdc.gov

A branch of the U.S. Department of Health and Human Services, the CDC serves as the national focus for developing and applying disease prevention and control, environmental health, and health promotion and education activities. An A–Z index, fact sheets on epilepsy, and links to resources and articles such as "Public Health and Epilepsy" are all available through its Web site.

Citizens United for Research in Epilepsy (CURE)
730 N. Franklin St.
Ste. 104
Chicago, IL 60610
(800) 765-7118
fax: (312) 255-1809
www.cureepilepsy.org

CURE is a volunteer-based nonprofit organization dedicated to finding a cure for epilepsy by raising funds for research and by increasing awareness of the prevalence and the devastation of this disease. Through its advocacy efforts, CURE has helped to raise federal funding on epilepsy research from $68 million to over $100 million so far. CURE's Web site provides up-to-date information on epilepsy research news, facts about epilepsy, and personal stories of those affected by the disorder.

Epilepsy Foundation
8301 Professional Pl.
Landover, MD
20785-7223
(800) 332-1000
fax: (301) 577-2684
www.epilepsy
foundation.org

Founded in 1967 as the Epilepsy Foundation of America, the Epilepsy Foundation is a national volunteer agency dedicated to the welfare of the more than 3 million people in the United States with epilepsy and their families. The organization works to ensure that people who have seizures are able to participate in all life experiences; to improve how people with epilepsy are perceived, accepted, and valued in society; and to promote research for a cure. Its Web site includes links to a resource center, archived news releases, congressional testimony, and fact sheets such as "Genetics and Epilepsy" and "The Scope of Epilepsy and Seizures in America."

Epilepsy Therapy Project
PO Box 742
Middleburg, VA
20118
(540) 687-8077
fax: (540) 687-8066
www.epilepsy.com

The Epilepsy Therapy Project is a nonprofit corporation that aims to overcome funding gaps and other roadblocks that slow the progress of new epilepsy therapies from the lab to the patient. Acting as both a catalyst and a clearinghouse for innovative research and the early commercialization of new therapies, the Epilepsy Therapy Project brings together financial resources, scientific insights, and business expertise from leading academic and industry participants. Myriad resources are available at its Web site, including the multichaptered booklets *All About Epilepsy and Seizures* and *Living with Epilepsy,* as well as links to clinical trials and a community forum.

Finding a Cure for Epilepsy and Seizures (FACES)
223 E. Thirty-fourth St.
New York, NY 10016
(646) 558-0900
fax: (646) 385-7163
http://faces.med.nyu
.edu

FACES is a nonprofit organization affiliated with New York University's Langone Medical Center and the NYU Comprehensive Epilepsy Center. Founded by a group of parents, patients, and doctors in 1994, FACES seeks to improve the quality of life for all people affected by epilepsy through research, education and awareness, and community-building events. Its Web site offers links to educational videos, a news archive, and research articles such as "Can You Eat Your Way to Seizure Control? The Ketogenic and Atkins Diet for Epilepsy."

International Bureau for Epilepsy (IBE)
11 Priory Hall,
Stillorgan
Dublin 18 Ireland
+353 1 210-8850
fax: +353 1 210-8450
www.ibe-epilepsy.org

The International Bureau for Epilepsy was established in 1961 as an organization of laypersons and professionals interested in the medical and nonmedical aspects of epilepsy. The IBE addresses such social problems as education, employment, insurance, driver's license restrictions, and public awareness. The Bureau also works in close liaison with the International League against Epilepsy (ILAE), an organization of professionals involved in the medical and scientific issues of epilepsy. The IBE publishes the *International Epilepsy News,* a quarterly magazine, and the *Travellers Handbook for People with Epilepsy,* a downloadable booklet.

International League Against Epilepsy (ILAE)
Avenue Jules
Bordetlaan 142
B-1140 Evere
Brussels, Belgium
+32 (0) 2 761-1647
fax: +32 (0) 2 761-1699
www.ilae.org

The ILAE is the world's preeminent association of physicians and other health professionals working to provide the highest quality of care and well-being for those afflicted with epilepsy and other related seizure disorders. The league aims to disseminate knowledge about epilepsy, to promote research and education, and to improve services and care for patients with epilepsy. Its Web site features the Worldwide Epilepsy Resource Directory, the International Anti-epileptic Drug Database, and links to brochures such as *Epilepsy in the Workplace.*

National Association of Epilepsy Centers (NAEC)
5575 Wayzata Blvd.
Ste. 200
Minneapolis, MN
55416
(888) 525-6232
fax: (952) 525-1560
www.naec-epilepsy.org

NAEC is a nonprofit trade association with a membership of more than one hundred specialized epilepsy centers in the United States. Founded in 1987 by physician leaders committed to setting a national agenda for quality epilepsy care, NAEC educates public and private policy makers and regulators about appropriate patient care standards, reimbursement, and medical services policies. With the goal of no seizures and no side effects, the NAEC strives to make high-quality health care available and affordable for epilepsy patients across the country. The Web site provides answers to commonly asked questions and links to additional resources on epilepsy.

National Institute of Neurological Disorders and Stroke (NINDS)
PO Box 5801
Bethesda, MD 20824
(800) 352-9424 or
(301) 496-5751
www.ninds.nih.gov

A branch of the U.S. National Institutes of Health, NINDS conducts, fosters, and guides research on the causes, prevention, diagnosis, and treatment of neurological disorders and stroke. It also provides grants-in-aid to public and private institutions and individuals in fields related to its areas of interest. Included at the NINDS Web site are an index of neurological disorders and an epilepsy information page.

People Against Childhood Epilepsy (PACE)
7 East Eighty-fifth St.
Ste. A3
New York, NY 10028
(212) 665-7223
fax: (212) 327-3075
www.paceusa.org

PACE is a nonprofit organization founded in 1996 by a group of parents in response to their experiences in caring for the medical, social, developmental, educational, and emotional needs of children with epilepsy. Its fund-raising efforts support advances in medical research on epilepsy and help to provide information and support to families with children who have epilepsy. PACE's Web site provides a list of books, videos, and other publications, as well as a link to Epilepsytalk, an online discussion group.

FOR FURTHER READING

Books

Richard Appleton and Anthony Marson, *Epilepsy: The Facts*. New York: Oxford University Press, 2009.

Thomas R. Browne and Gregory L. Holmes, *Handbook of Epilepsy*. Hagerstown, MD: Lippincott and Wilkins, 2008.

Stacey Chillemi, *Epilepsy—You're Not Alone: How to Cope with the Disorder*. Raleigh, NC: Lulu.com, 2006.

Orrin Devinsky, *Epilepsy: A Patient and Family Guide*. New York: Demos Medical, 2007.

Sally Fletcher, *The Challenge of Epilepsy*. Scarsdale, NY: Aura, 2004.

Kaarkuzhali Babu Krishnamurthy et al., *Epilepsy in Our Lives: Women Living with Epilepsy*. New York: Oxford University Press, 2007.

Ilo E. Leppik, *Epilepsy: A Guide to Balancing Your Life*. New York: Demos Medical, 2007.

Stuart McCallum, *Beyond My Control: One Man's Struggle with Epilepsy, Seizure Surgery, and Beyond*. www.iuniverse.com, 2008.

Georgia P. Montouris and John M. Pellock, *Epilepsy on Our Terms: Stories by Children with Seizures and Their Parents*. New York: Oxford University Press, 2007.

Carl Reiter, *Epilepsy: The Complete Handbook*. Raleigh, NC: Lulu.com, 2008.

Markus Reuber, Christian E. Elger, and Steven C. Schachter, *Epilepsy Explained: A Book for People Who Want to Know More*. New York: Oxford University Press, 2009.

Steven C. Schachter, ed., *Epilepsy in Our Words: Personal Accounts of Living with Seizures*. New York: Oxford University Press, 2007.

Simon P. Shorvon, *Handbook of Epilepsy Treatment*. Hoboken, NJ: Wiley-Blackwell, 2005.

Andrew N. Wilner, *Epilepsy, 199 Answers: A Doctor Responds to His Patients' Questions*. 3rd ed. New York: Demos Medical, 2008.

Periodicals

Doug Brunk, "Art Provides Window on Epilepsy Experience," *Clinical Psychiatry News*, March 2007.

Melissa Daly, "Hearing Music Gave Me Seizures," *Cosmopolitan*, August 2008.

Economist, "Quieting the Brain, Opening the Mind," February 5, 2005.

Victoria Stagg Elliott, "Epilepsy Care Goal Shifting to No Seizures, Not Just Fewer Ones," *American Medical News*, September 8, 2008.

Guardian (Manchester, UK), "My Near Death Period: HIV, Epilepsy, Comas and Memory Loss Haven't Stopped Mark Ravenhill Writing," March 26, 2008.

Ben Harder, "Ketones to the Rescue," *Science News*, December 13, 2003.

Gardiner Harris and Benedict Carey, "FDA Finds Increase in Suicide Symptoms for Patients Using Seizure Medications," *New York Times*, February 1, 2008.

Bonnie Henry, "Poet Explores Profound Effects of Epilepsy," *Arizona Daily Star* (Tucson), August 24, 2006.

Christiana Liu et al., "A Prospective Study: Growth and Nutritional Status of Children Treated with the Ketogenic Diet," *Journal of the American Dietetic Association*, June 2003.

Michael Mason, "Dead Men Walking," *Discover*, February 23, 2007.

Robert Mitchum, "Seizures Are a Relatively Common Medical Phenomenon," *Chicago Tribune*, July 31, 2007.

Patricia Osborne Shafer, "Seizures and Teens," *Exceptional Parent*, July 2007.

Penny Wark, "'It's Like Someone's Turned Off the TV,'" *Times* (London), September 1, 2008.

Jen Waters, "Taking Epilepsy Down a Notch," *Washington Times*, July 4, 2006.

INDEX